HELL

ON

EARTH

Pastor Olabisi Obideyi

ISBN: 9781466473881
Scripture quotations are from the Holy Bible Authorized King James version, copyright ©1982 by Thomas Nelson.

Published by Divine Grace Enterprises Limited.

DIVINE GRACE
ENTERPRISE LIMITED.
"For with Grace Enterprise, nothing shall be impossible"

www.divinegraceenterprise.com
Cover Design by: Zoe Communications Limited.
Manuscript editing: Kit Olsen (United States of America).

Printed in the United States of America and the United Kingdom.

CONTENTS

ACKNOWLEDGEMENTS

thank the Lord God Almighty—the Father, the Son and the Holy Spirit, for enabling me to write this book for the proclamation of His Good Name.

I am blessed to use this opportunity to thank my immediate family. Beginning with my father, Enoch Oladejo Obideyi—for all his encouragement throughout the years, my son Temitope for his understanding, and my daughter Precious for her enduring patience and understanding toward me during the course of this writing.

My special thanks goes to all members of Freedom House International Ministries for their perseverance and support, especially during my most extremely difficult times. I would also like to extend my sincere gratitude to Pastor Wale Orelesi for his entire professional input and also to my sisters in the Lord: Jacqui Bweyame, Joyce Edoreh and Kit Olsen for their loving assistance with this book.

Finally my sincere gratitude goes to the God of Abraham, Isaac and Jacob—for blessing me with the encouragement of my readers, friends and all my supporters throughout the years. Knowing you are all a part of my life is a great source of inspiration to me. I pray that the ever-abiding grace of our Lord Jesus Christ, the love of God and the sweet fellowship of the Holy Spirit will continue to rest and abide with you all now and forevermore. Amen.

INTRODUCTION

From time immemorial countless people on earth have been engaged in affording the human race answers in regards to the question of how we came to exist on planet Earth. One of such answers suggest that we all came into existence as a result of a 'big bang' event that supposedly took place some billions of years back. The question however is: If no man has lived for up to a thousand years on earth, how could anyone be certain this is true? If all that an answer is only capable of producing is more questions, then the answer is by no means conclusive.

Most human beings in the world are generally occupied with coping with the challenges of daily life. Consequentially, the emphasis of such people often times is not so much to do with discovering how they came to be. With such a mindset, it is understandable why people would simply adopt an answer from the many that are available in the world without questioning. However, to settle for a false answer is to end up with a conviction that is no more than a major barrier to identifying and accepting the real *truth*.

The underlying effect of the several contradictory answers that are provided by those that have made it their business to do so is: confusion. Therefore, it is essential that we avoid the lethal effect of confusion by ensuring that we do not just accept things on face value. Many people today are promoters of beliefs—which they have accepted on face value. As a result, they are obsessively passionate about promoting or spreading something that they have no genuine insight as to what it is all about.

The fact is human beings are complex beings by nature. Just as we are complex as a matter of nature, so it is that our existence is a complex mystery that cannot be easily unravelled by any ideas that are naturally logical to us. To resolve the mysteries behind our human existence, we need to seek beyond the 'ordinarily visible' to the 'extraordinarily invisible'. We need to carefully consider all things, and in so doing ask ourselves whether the so-called answers from the experts are revelations from a higher source or mere human assumptions. We also need to consider from where the human answer providers derived their answers. Did they adopt those answers because they make perfect natural logical 'sense' even though they are of no spiritual 'sense' whatsoever? We need to begin our journey of finding the whole truth by asking ourselves questions that are bound to lead us to the whole answer. Unless we start by asking the right kind of questions, we will not find the true answers.

If we simply embrace a generalist answer to certain specific questions we have deep down in our minds, how can we be certain that the answers are the answers we truly need? If the earth pre-existed the physical man that dwells on it, then not only do we need answers concerning how man came to exist on earth, we also need answers regarding why and how the planet itself came into existence.

Life is all about purpose and unless we seek with a purposeful-mind, we will not find the whole truth concerning our existence. We can only begin to make sense of everything if we understand our life's purpose. To discover our purpose on earth we must start by asking:

"Who are we, how did we get here, where do we come from and where do we end up when we leave here"?

We need to ask: Are we only here on earth for the sake of habitation simply because earth is the only place in the galaxy that is suitable for our survival? If we say we are here for the sake of habitation, then does it mean it is up to us to treat ourselves and everything else we find on planet Earth as we please? Did we come from nothingness? If we answer yes, does it mean we are supreme in the galaxy and as such need only to operate within our own human constraints and regulations? If man is completely supreme, does it mean he has ultimate power and control over the entire universe? We need to ask whether life is all about what we can see with our ordinary eyes or are there other things or beings in existence that ordinary eyes cannot see? If we say life is all about natural and visible existence, does it mean our entire lifespan begins and ends in the natural?

We all came into the earth with nothing and we cannot take anything with us when we leave. The question then is: Are we only here to enjoy our planet in our timely existence, and after we have lived our lives disappear back into nothingness when our time is up? Most people will agree with me in saying that human life in this world is far from fun and games. Life on earth for many is a daily rat race of endless labour with nothing to show for it. Whilst on one hand, the minority controls earthly wealth and its resources living in excess of their needs. On the other hand, majority of the human population struggles to get by in the midst of serious, debilitating economic hardship. Rarely does a day go by that we do not hear of stories and news about economic hardship, death, war, famine, killer diseases and all kinds of terrible things happening to human beings across the world. Bearing this in mind, should we then conclude that the vast majority of humans merely exist on earth for the sake of suffering and nothing else?

If natural life is total existence, how do we explain the unequal results from our efforts? Why do some with little or no effort always seem to have their way, while some never seem to succeed in anything no matter how hard they try? Does it mean life on earth is just a gambling game, with just the very few destined to play and win, and the rest deemed to lose? If life in the world is the beginning and the end, is it not then proper that we all have equal access and rights to the riches and resources in our planet?

How then do we justify the fact that the world's surplus resources and wealth are all in the controlling hands of the minority? If we say the purpose of our existence on earth is to enjoy earthly wealth and resources, how will the deprived majority be recompensed for their own loss of enjoyment? Is it really a wise idea to only hope in the system of this world judging by the height of corruption that is at the heart of the several world systems? If world polices continue to produce a result of widening the gap between the poor and the rich instead of closing it, will there ever come a time when the whole of mankind would enjoy equal economical freedom? Based upon the self- destructive nature of mankind, could we truly say man is independently in control of his planetary affairs or are there external forces behind the scenes motivating human actions on earth? If life begins and ends on earth, does it mean justice for the entire human race is all down to a world system that is in itself unjust?

The more we ask these kinds of questions the more we will see that there is more to life than meets our eyes. We live in a world of so many questions and no obvious realistic answers and unless we look beyond what our 'natural' eyes can see, we will continue to miss the entire point of our existence. If we are to make sense of our human existence, we must indeed start our quest for the truth by finding the answers to the basic question of how we came into existence. It is only when we can ascertain our true roots that everything else will begin to make sense. To discover the real truth about how we came into existence, we must seek our answers from the right source. No human being can find the answers to who they are or where they are going, unless they look beyond the ordinarily visible to the extraordinarily invisible. Every being on earth is on a journey to discover who they are. If you do not know who you are, you cannot know where you are and if you have no idea where you are, you simply cannot find your way to where you need to be.

Our human existence on earth is in fact a secret and no one can reveal the secret of our existence to us except God, the self-existing Creator Uncreated. Prior to God opening my spiritual eyes, I was so certain that I knew exactly who I was and where I was headed. I considered myself a true Christian and thought I knew everything there was to know about God, my existence and my Christian faith. I argued blindly about my faith and about every other subject area pertaining to human existence. I saw myself as a wise person full of life knowledge. Even though I considered myself a devoted Christian, I never saw God in mind as One to have a personal relationship with, and despite my conviction that I was sufficiently religious and therefore godly, I always felt very confused and empty on the inside for some unexplainable reasons.

It was this feeling of emptiness that prompted me to seek answers away from the visible man to the Invisible God. Fortunately and to God, be all the glory, my soul search paid off toward the end of 2003. Through various stages of revelations beginning from October 2003, God started to unravel the mysteries of our world to me. As He began to open my eyes to see the truth, I realised that my once thought wisdom was nothing more than ignorance and foolishness.

The testimony you are about to read from Chapter One of this book is my testimony and account of God's end-time revelations to me. God revealed the hidden secrets of the human world and beyond to me, to reaffirm to mankind that hell is an invisible prison-realm at the centre of the earth. Unless a soul enters the only doorway out of hell before Judgement Day, that soul will be imprisoned in hell fire to suffer for eternity. The only exit out of hell and as the only door, the only gateway to eternal life in heaven is Christ Jesus—Lord and Saviour, Creator and Redeemer of mankind.

I pray God will open your eyes of understanding as you begin to read the revelation account that is in this book—to clearly see that Christ is the only door to heaven. The only Way, the only Truth and only Life. I also pray Christ as the Door, guides you by His special grace to enter into Him and enable you to rest and abide with Him everlastingly to the glory of the self-existing—Creator Uncreated God the Father, Son and Holy Spirit. Amen.

HELL ON EARTH

CHAPTER ONE
THE BEGINNING OF REVELATIONS

"For we wrestle not against flesh and blood, but against principalities, against powers, against rulers of darkness of this world, against spiritual wickedness in high places".

—Ephesians 6:12

With spiritual hindsight and insight, I am now convinced that my spiritual journey of revelations actually began long before my conscious awakening—which took place in the year 2004. My spiritual journey started in the year 1995 with some major significant dreams. Prior to having these significant dreams, my dream world was always a very busy one, full off all kinds of strange pictures and faces. To avoid worrying over the meaning of these dreams, I always tried not to attach too much importance to them. However, on several occasions I would reach out for my Bible in the middle of the night to place it under my pillow after having one of these dreams—nightmares. This was the main use I had for my Bible then and it seemed to work at all times, because soon after I placed my Bible under my pillow I would fall back asleep. When the nightmares became too frequent, I made underneath my pillow a permanent home for my Bible and strangely enough, having the Bible stationed permanently under my pillow afforded me some sort of sleep confidence.

In the year 1995, I had a memorable dream that I believe had some significant meaning that went beyond my normal, busy mortal dream life. In this dream I found myself somewhere above the clouds and right in front of me were three, beyond my comprehension—powerful looking handsome men. They were so extraordinarily unusual and none like them on earth. They were wearing huge white robes. The one in the middle was sitting whilst the other two were standing beside him on their feet—one on the left and the other on the right. It was as if they summoned me there to tell me something or remind me of something. However, I was so fascinated by their amazing beauty that I did not hear or understand what was being said. The one in the middle did most of the talking and the other two smiled at me a lot. After the one in the middle finished speaking, he stretched out his hand toward me and from his hand came a staff to mine. Before I could ask any questions, the three men disappeared and I saw a staircase leading all the way down from the place that is above the clouds to the open earth space.

With the Staff in hand, I descended from the stairs all the way down and when I got to the bottom of the stairs, I found myself right in the midst of a large crowd. It was as if they knew I was coming because they appeared really desperate and impatient for my arrival. As I stepped down from the last step, the crowd surged toward me from every angle and I became scared. It seemed as though they were going to squeeze the life right out of me. Out of fear I started running away from them. The more I ran the closer they were getting to me. Still very afraid—but tremendously relieved, I woke up from the dream. I knew at the time that the dream must have some significance, but I had no idea what it could be.

In the following year, I had another dream which I also

thought must be of great importance. In this dream, I saw a man glowing like light, standing face to face with me. The man taught me a prayer and told me to recite the prayer when I wake-up and also that I should not worry because all is well. The prayer was a short one and it went something like this:

"Thank You O Lord for all that You have done for me. Forgive me O Lord my sins. Continue O Lord to have mercy upon me so that I may rest and abide with You forever. In Jesus' Name I have prayed".

The moment I woke up, I wrote down the prayer and recited it. From that day onward, I would recite that prayer whenever I felt down or saddened, and I would always feel relieved afterward. Whilst all this was going on, my human (natural) life was not what I considered as fantastic, but it was not what many would consider terrible either. In the year 1997, I realised my lifelong ambition to study Law and soon after completing my degree, I managed to secure a job that same year. I was not long in my job before I got promoted and soon after, my husband and I got a breakthrough to purchase our own house. We moved into our new house in the year 2000 and in the following year, I got another job closer to our new home with a higher salary. However, although everything seemed to be going according to plan, for some reason I was deeply unhappy and did not know why. By the time I started my new job in 2001, I could not wait to get yet another job. What I had thought would make me happily fulfilled did not. Often times, once I had achieved my desired goal, I would immediately think of pursuing something else, and this need to keep on pursuing one thing or the other was like an addictive problem I was suffering from for which there is no cure.

Even though I considered myself a faithful Christian, my spiritual life appeared to be non-existent. I did not know how to pray nor did I know where to find anything in the Bible. My main use of the Bible was placing it under my pillow to protect me against nightmares. Occasionally, I would recite the prayer that I got in my dream back in 1996, but unlike before it did not satisfy me the way it had before. I had the feeling I needed to be doing something more and was mostly frustrated for not specifically knowing what it was that I needed to do more of. I felt so empty and void inside.

To try and help this situation I became a regular churchgoer. I thought going to church regularly would help, but it did not. To make matters worse, I felt no one could understand how I was feeling since I could not even understand it myself, let alone able to explain it to anyone to make them understand. To worsen the situation further, it was as if my good run was fully over. I had reached a point where nothing I did worked anymore and all doors of progression seemed to be firmly shut. In the midst of these mounting problems in my every day life, I became very depressed about everything. I hated every single thing about my life and hated the world even more; which as far as I was concerned is full of nothing but injustice, inequality and unfairness.

To heighten my social image profile, I had taken on cigarette smoking and drinking some years back. However, in the thick of this inner-struggle, my depression escalated. Indulging in smoking and drinking became the very height of my comfort zone and no longer a mere expression of my believed social status. Therefore, I considered anyone who would suggest that I give up drinking and smoking as my enemy. I could not think of anything to replace my drinking and smoking habit with and the more I saw cigarette smoking and heavy alcohol consumption as my only comfort, the more I wanted to deepen my relationship with alcohol and cigarette smoking. Most of the time I felt trapped doing what I did not enjoy and this made me even sadder because I could not envision any possible way out.

I had always enjoyed helping people and felt somehow very frustrated for not being in the position I ideally wish to be in, to be able help people as much as I desire to. Consequently, in my frustrations, I became an emotional wreck and was very tearful most of the time for no apparent reason. Life on earth started to feel more like everyday hell. The more I looked at the world the more it appeared as a prison, and seeing the world this way made me feel more helpless and hopeless. The more hopeless I became the more I began to see taking my life as the only way out from the world. I had an unexplainable burden and felt extremely frustrated that no one seemed to be available anywhere to help shift or share my burden. My life became a vicious cycle of repeated daily routines. Everything became increasingly frustrating and monotonous. I felt like I was in search of something but the worst aspect was I had no idea what it was I was looking for. I felt completely alone and it was as if no one was available to help me.

The more I deliberated on my life the more depressed I became. The more depressed I got the more I kept on thinking I was better off dead, than to continue to live in a world that was now appearing as a hell-hole full of many sorrows. The strangest thing in all of this was that everyone around me looked up to me and saw me as someone with great potentials. As a result, I felt I had no one around me that I could speak to, who would understand what I was going through. I felt somehow strangely isolated and the more isolated I felt, the more God began to appear as an enemy rather than a friend.

My feelings of depression reached a crucial point in the year 2003. From the beginning of that year I started thinking I might have breast cancer and that I was going to die from it. Even though I had been thinking that death was the best way out, the reality of dying from breast cancer really scared me. I walked around suffering in silence with the thought that I might have breast cancer. Because of the fear that I might just discover that I have breast cancer if I were to consult my doctor, I refused to see the doctor to have me examined. At a point when my inner-suffering became too unbearable, I decided it was best to speak to a friend about my fear that I might have breast cancer, and it was she who encouraged me to see my doctor. When I finally plucked up the courage and went to see the doctor, he gave me the all clear and assured me that I do not have breast cancer. However, the thought that I might have cancer or could still have it refused to go away. At this point even though I was walking around pretending everything was perfectly okay, I felt as if I had died on the inside. As my feelings of tortuous depression continually worsened, my moods of sorrow reached an unbearable level to the point where I became desperate for help—more than ever before in my life.

The turnaround in my life leading to greater revelation experiences came about in October 2003. By the month of October I had gotten so distressed and frustrated to the extent that all I wanted most of the time was to be by myself and cry my eyes out. Everything seemed to be going the opposite direction and things got tougher and tougher instead of getting better. I could not help but blame God for everything that had gone wrong in my life because as far as I was concerned, He has all the power but so far it seemed like He had refused to do anything to help me get out of my desperate situation.

Although I had seemingly considered God as my number one enemy all along, it reached a stage one Saturday night in October 2003 when I realised I needed God more than ever, if I was going to figure out what was going on in my life. I sought God's face that night and asked for His help in a way that I had never done before. I wanted to know Him for who He is and not for the things that I used to seek Him for previously, which were all to do with my wants and desires in the world. I began by asking many questions such as: "Why am I here on this earth, what is my purpose and does God ever listen to me at all"?

I realised how hopeless and helpless I had become and wondered if God could see just how hopeless and helpless I was. I begged Him to come to my rescue if He was hearing me because I was tired and in desperate need of His help. I asked Him to forgive me if I had offended Him in any way and pleaded with Him that I was at breaking point and desperate for any form of breakthrough assistance that He could give me. Life had no meaning to me and I wanted to know the meaning of life. I cried so much that night to the extent that when I awoke the following day, which was a Sunday, it was with a severe headache and blocked nose.

In my belief of a Christian life, I had always equated serving God with attending church and as such, I became a regular churchgoer along the way in order to convince God to help me out of my troubles. However, in the midst of my unending trials, I had since stopped attending church before the said night of October 2003. I stopped attending church altogether as I could no longer see any point in serving a God who seems unprepared to use His power to give me a breakthrough from my life struggles. As result of no longer attending church on Sundays, I often spent my Sunday's time mostly in front of the television and in between watching television, focusing myself on worrying about my miserable life.

Following my night of plea with God, I woke up the morning after which as I said was a Sunday, to worry as usual on the events of my life. After I had finished my usual chores, I decided to watch the television as I normally do on Sundays. I switched the television on to the news channel and as usual, it was the same horror stories. The news was all about death, war and one disaster after another. I changed the channel after a few minutes of watching as it was making me feel even more depressed and hopeless about my entire life. I turned to one of the Christian channels and found that a preacher I had listened to a number of times was in the middle of a sermon. I was about changing the channel again to another channel when I heard the preacher mention the word 'purpose'. So, I decided to listen.

The main theme of the preacher's message was that; God is a God of promises and that if we search through the Bible, we would find His promises for us. He mentioned that we should all be positive in our thinking and that when we are down, we should search through the Bible for God's promises. He said that when we read the Bible, we should form a habit of highlighting God's promises and know them by heart in order to encourage ourselves. The message cheered me up a bit and given the state of my mind at that time, I could well do with some cheering up. As I continued listening to the message, I kept wondering about the biblical promises the preacher mentioned and also how they related to me.

After I had finished listening to the sermon, I decided to search the Bible for the promises the preacher spoke about. The only thing I was familiar with in the Bible was Psalm 23 and when I picked up my Bible that day, I had no clue where to start. Due to my lack of biblical knowledge, finding the promises was like finding a needle out of a haystack. However, I was desperate to find the promises the preacher mentioned even if it meant reading the Bible from the beginning to the very end. In desperate mind search of biblical promises, I opened the first book, Genesis and began to read from verse one. By the time I reached verse three something amazing happened to me that was beyond my comprehension. For some strange reason, Genesis, chapter One, verses one to three[1] meant so much to me and just from reading them, I felt like someone had lifted a veil off my eyes. I heard a voice whispering some words to me and these words were soothing to my ears. Although I could not pinpoint what had actually happened, I knew something good had happened or better still, was about to happen.

After this unexplainable experience, I suddenly became a lot more interested in praying, but no longer for the worldly things I use to ask God for previously. My prayer life became more and more focused on a relationship with God. I prayed that He would draw me closer to Him, reveal my purpose to me and help me fulfil it for His glory. Miraculously, I stopped smoking and drinking alcohol. Also for reasons unknown to me as of that time, I became very interested in spending time reading the Bible. Since I had no idea where to find anything, I would

---

[1]Genesis Chapter 1: 1-3: In the beginning God created the heaven and the earth. And the earth was without form, and void; and darkness was upon the face of the deep. And the Spirit of God moved upon the face of the waters. And God said, Let there be light: and there was light.

simply open the Bible and read whichever page I randomly came across. Amazingly, I usually land on a page full of Words of promises from God and the more I read these Words of promises, the more I look forward to opening and reading my Bible again and again.

In February 2004 I had another experience that put everything in a higher perspective. Following my 2003 experience, I had daily continued to read any biblical chapter I randomly open and I always follow up with a little prayer to God for Him to draw me closer to Him. One day in the month of February 2004, instead of randomly opening a Bible page to read any chapter that I found as I had done previously, I strangely felt prompted to open my Bible to the book of Acts, chapter two and read it. After I had finished reading, I decided to say my usual little prayer. However, as I opened my mouth to pray, instead of saying my usual words of prayer, I burst out in tears and no matter how hard I tried I just couldn't stop crying. I cried so much to the point of having a blocked nose. As I was crying I started singing and could not stop singing. I repeatedly sang two songs. The first one begins with "I love you Lord" and the second song I mainly sang the chorus:

"Lord I give you my heart, I give you my soul, I live for You alone, every breath that I take, every moment I am awake, Lord have Your Way with me".

As I continued singing, I suddenly started falling down all over the place as if hit by a whirlwind force and each time I fell, I would rise up only to fall down again. After several falls, I decided to remain flat on the floor. I have no idea of how long I was on the floor, but when I stood up again, I opened my mouth and I started to speak in 'tongues'. The amazing thing was that I understood every word. Translated, it went like this:

"Woman thou art loosed. Rejoice, today for I have fully delivered you from the claws of Lucifer. Your heart was hardened and I had to circumcise it. Now in a good circumcised heart you are totally free from all shackles and bondage. In total freedom, go into the world and proclaim the Gospel and I will be with you even to the end of days."

When the interpretation came to me I could not curtail my joy. I started jumping up and down with intense excitement, repeatedly shouting, **"I am free, Jesus is Lord"**! I felt like calling a press conference just to say to the whole world, **"Jesus is Lord, God is real, and I know it"**. I felt totally free and though I could not explain this new found freedom, I just knew I was free from something that had been compressing me all of my life. It was my personal 'Damascus Road' experience.

Soon after this encounter, I started hearing the 'Voice' of the Lord and amazingly, it was as if we had always been in regular communication. It did not feel strange at all to engage in conversation with Him. Instead, it felt soothingly pleasant. The first task He gave me was to set up a ministry called, Freedom House International Ministries and that the word, 'Freedom' means to be *free in all dominion*. When I told Him I had no idea how to run a church and that I also did not have any Bible knowledge, He told me, "I know everything that you know and everything that you do not know".

He also said I should not worry because all that I needed to know He would teach me. True to His Word, God became my daily Bible Teacher. He started from Genesis, the first book of the Bible. After a short while of His teaching me, He told me it was time to start the ministry and instructed me to invite everyone I know for the first service. God gave me an amazing ministry vision and having seen all that He had shown me, I was very enthusiastic to begin my godly ministerial mission journey.

I obeyed God's instruction and called the few people that I knew for the service—mostly old drinking and smoking pals and a few work colleagues. I was amazed when seven people turned up on the first day of fellowship. Although I called the people that I knew in obedience to God's instruction, I was not really expecting anyone to take me seriously. God gave me a sermon to give to the seven people that came and as far as I was concerned, the church was on the move.

From the look of things, I was highly expectant of a quick congregational growth and in line with my expectations, overly joyful at how things appear to be speedily progressing. I was convinced in my mind that if seven people could turn up at the first service, those seven people having witnessed the glory of God would certainly be returning the following Sunday and will most likely invite someone along with them to come and share in the unique experience they've had at the first service. Based upon my calculations of likely rate of congregation growth, I began foreseeing us soon moving from a house fellowship into a large auditorium and for the first time in my life, everything was looking so good. God was on my side as my Teacher and unlike before, I felt fulfilled doing what He was now leading me to do.

However, what happened next was just the opposite of what I had hoped or expected would happen. My feelings of euphoric elation were quickly challenged. To my surprise, not only did I not have fourteen people the following Sunday in accordance with my estimate of each person inviting someone along, I had seven minus one person. The Sunday after that, I again ended up with another reduction and this reduction continued every subsequent Sunday, until one Sunday nobody turned up. When everyone stopped coming, I was disappointed but not devastated. God made me to understand that all that was happening was to perfect my faith in Him, and He reassured me that with Him all things are possible. In addition, He said my ministry work had not even started because there are lots of things I am yet to understand. Since it wasn't in my plan to be a Pastor in the first place, I saw no reason to feel devastated when it began to seem as if the ministry would never take off as God had promised it would.

In the meantime, although it looked as if my ministry life was over even before it began, God started revealing some amazing things to me through dreams, actual conversations with Him and by visions. In one of such visions, He took me back in time to the day of Christ's crucifixion. As they were nailing Him to the Cross I felt like I was being crucified with Him and I could actually feel the nails go through my feet and hands. After His crucifixion, I saw Christ covered with blood. He had on His head a crown of thorns and He was walking on a sea of blood. He had blood dripping all over Him. Immediately afterward I saw Him again, but this time He was walking on crystal clear water full of a beauty beyond description. Although His shape was like that of a man, He had a bright, glowing, beautiful appearance. As He was walking on the crystal clear water I saw that He was actually carrying me in His arms. I also noticed that as He was carrying me along, the clear waters surrounding us were stunningly radiant. I heard Him say: "Fear not, for you are safe with Me and I will never leave nor forsake you".

With highly significant visions now part of my everyday life, God as my Teacher continued to teach me the Scriptures in the most amazing way. Besides teaching me the Scriptures, He also instructed me to undertake different types of fasts. Before my Holy Spirit encounter, I had never been able to fast—mainly because the first thing I usually reached out for in the morning was a cigarette. During lent, I would sometimes have the urge to fast to satisfy my religious 'conscience'. However, it seemed there was never a right day for me to fast. I always had one excuse after another why not to begin fasting on the day I planned to. I usually ended up opting to delay my fast from one next day to another. Inexplicably, for some strange reason I found that my craving for cigarettes and food to be at an unusually irritable and irresistible height the moment I would wake-up on the day I planned to begin my fasts. The moment I had smoked cigarettes and eaten, I would then postpone starting the fast until the following day and my following day postponement never seemed to end!

However, when God began instructing me to fast, fasting became the easiest thing for me to do. I would have no urge for food and I would always fast whichever way He instructed me to. Strangely enough, I noted that when I started my heavy fasting sessions, my dream world became what I call: Battlefront Galactic. The moment I closed my eyes, I would immediately find myself in a dream world filled with intense warfare. As dream world battle became a daily occurrence in my life, I very quickly went from cold turkey to becoming a prayer warrior. I would awake from a dreamland battle and engage in some heavy casting and binding sessions and the more I fasted and prayed, the fiercer the battle became in my dream world.

God became my entire focus and He often assured me not to worry about what my dream life had become, because it is an evidence of my spiritual awakening. He added: "To be a warrior is to have victory in all realms, including the realm of dreams".

Supernaturally, I was having a perfect and wonderful relationship with God. However, it was as if my perfect relationship with God was only working to worsen things for me in the natural. Aside from my dreamland battles, I had all sorts of problems imaginable and unimaginable, ranging from serious marital problems to crippling financial struggles. I cried a lot, but strangely no longer because I was sad or sorrowful, but mainly for the fact that I was so overjoyed and overwhelmed with God's love toward me. God's endless, amazing love for me made up for everything I was going through and fasting and praying became my lifestyle.

I felt so privileged and appreciative that the Most High God of the universe had chosen to reveal Himself to a common mortal like myself. The more God revealed to me, the sorrier I felt for my fellow human beings. Most of the time I would supplicate unto God, pleading with Him to show the same kind of mercy to my fellow humans that He had shown me—whom I could now see mostly as lost and confused souls. In my everyday relationship with God, I discovered a side of God that is hidden from humans. I found out that God is incredibly wonderful, gentle, loving and merciful. From seeing God this way, I always saw a need to humble myself before Him. Having experienced God's love on a daily basis, my desire to be closer to Him in my relationship with Him increased day by day. With His daily Holy Spirit presence in my life, God's love for me became very real in my everyday life. I found it mostly amazing, that even though God is able to force me into submission, He instead prefers to love me into submission unto Himself.

My appreciation and respect for God's honour increased daily and during moments of prayer or worship, I often ended up shedding lots of tears. Not in sadness, but in joyful appreciation of His overwhelming love for me. The more I experienced God's love, the more the difficulties I was going through looked trivial. Just as God promised that He would never leave nor forsake me, He was always there to encourage and enable me to rise above everything that people were now throwing at me from every angle. Through daily expression of His comforting love toward me, the worst days ended up being the best days for me spiritually because on such days—God's comfort toward me was even more expounded. The more comfort I received from Him, the closer I wanted to be with Him. The closer I grew to Him, the more I felt His love for me. Despite my undergoing immense trials and tribulations, I felt a new kind of joy and contentment beyond my human comprehension.

As days and months passed, my relationship with God grew from strength to strength. On a daily basis, God engaged me in so much writing that I usually carried a notepad with me everywhere I went because of the unending urge I had to keep jotting down His Words to me. However, just as I was beginning to fully enjoy the endless comforting voice and love of God, I began to hear other threatening and vicious voices. Conversing with God felt as if I had a strong signal link from earth to heaven that made it possible for me each day to hear God so clearly. However, I realised that most of the time when I had the urge to pray, I would end up getting signal interruption in the form of voices saying all kinds of negative and scary things such as: I should kill myself, there is no God and so on and so forth.

I often used to get scared whenever I heard these threatening, negative voices and I soon discovered that scaring me not to pray was their intended aim. Thanks be to God, He always overrode my feelings of fear by enabling me to fire out the right prayer words, and once I started praying, the voices would stop. Without any prior spiritual knowledge or experience, I was for quite some time baffled by the sudden shift from the soothing Words of God to the wicked voice attacks of evil.

I enjoyed praying for people and wished people would change for the sake of goodness. God always encouraged me to fast and pray for others and seek goodness for others. When I asked God about the negative voices, His answer to me was this:

To overcome false fear, which is a weapon of the spirits of darkness, one must know the secrets of evil realms and to know the secrets of evil realms is to prevail over entire evil. Complete knowledge of life is knowledge of good and evil and to know good and evil and choose good, is to be good on deeds. To see and defeat evil is to recognise the strength of goodness. Where there is a conflict between good and evil, good always prevails because good and evil always work together for goodness sake.

I had previously thought that I knew exactly what constituted good and evil. Therefore, when God started saying there is greater invisible evil, which is beyond human comprehension and that this evil is what Man is up against, I was not sure what He meant. Evil as far as I was concerned started and ended with things like rape, murder and beyond such things I could not think of any kind of greater evil that human beings can be up against. Prior to my closeness to God, I had heard of stories of spiritual evil attacks on people but I had never taken such stories seriously. I saw myself as an ordinary person and could not think of any reason why anyone visible or invisible would want to attack someone as ordinary as myself. Besides, with God's goodness now so visible to me, I could not even begin to think of any form of evil in existence. However, God always said: "I will reveal the secrets of life to you one day and when I do, everything will become a lot clearer to you".

CHAPTER TWO
HELL REVEALED

"And they overcame him by the blood of the Lamb, and by the word of their testimony; and they loved not their lives unto death. Therefore rejoice, ye heavens and ye that dwell in them. Woe to the inhabiters of the earth and of the seal for the devil is come down unto you, having great wrath, because he knoweth that he hath but a short time".
—Revelation 12:11-12

My relationship with God waxed stronger on a daily basis as He continued teaching me His spiritual knowledge. One morning toward the end of the month of July in the year 2004, at a point when I thought my relationship with God could not be better; I woke up to discover that this day was to be an unusual one. Although I was still in the world physically, I was actually seeing a realm of a world that I had not seen or known of beforehand. It was as if I had landed in a world totally hidden from the physical world we know and live in. But at the same time still living in the same world we all know and live in as humans.

The invisible, yet totally now visible to me, seemed like the real world and it looked scarily different from what I had known the visible world to be all my life. To make matters worse, the atmosphere stank terribly—like nothing I'd smelt before on the face of the earth. The smell was so choking that all I wanted to do was hold my breath to prevent myself from breathing in the terrible bad smell. When I looked outside from my living room window, I discovered that the faces of the passers-by no longer looked like those of human beings. Instead of normal human looking beings, I saw creatures of all shapes and sizes in all kinds of different colours.

At first, I thought I was having a very bad nightmare and hoped to wake-up from it any moment. I decided to put the television on and as soon as it came on, I immediately realised that I was not dreaming and that everything I was seeing was as real as it could ever get! The first thing I noted once I turned the television on was that although the television was transmitting pictures as usual, none of the images coming from the television set appeared to be human in appearance. I had lost consciousness of time as we know it and to make matters worse, I began hearing what sounded like billions of voices hurling all manner of abuses at me all at once.

For some reason I was unable to sit down or remain still. All I wanted to do was pace up and down the house. I noted in particular that each time I walked past the large mirror on the wall of our living room, I would hear a loud voice say, "Now you are dead and ugly, do us a favour kill yourself and if you do not, we will destroy you". I tried to ignore all the weird things I was seeing and hearing, attempting as much as possible to behave and act as if everything was 'normal'. However, the more I tried to behave normal the louder the voices got. As I continued pacing up and down, I heard a voice say, "Welcome to the world of the dead and to the battle of Armageddon". I had heard the word 'Armageddon' before. However, I could not understand why an ordinary person like myself was now suddenly engaged in this battle of 'Armageddon'. Worst of all, it was as if God had abandoned me and I was now all on my own.

As I kept pacing up and down trying to figure out what was going on, I heard another voice say, "The battle of Armageddon is a fierce battle and no human being can win because no man can overcome death in the land of the dead". I quickly discovered that the only weapons I had in this battle were words and if I did not have the right word to counteract my opponent's words, it would soon be game over for me. Every word of the opponent was like a piercing arrow. However, I realised that whenever I opened my mouth to counteract their evil words, I had just the right word coming forth from my mouth. I walked up and down the house uttering words of mystery, I felt had to be given to me by God.

Even though I was unsure in my human consciousness what was happening, it was somehow evident to me that God had been preparing me all along just for this moment. Nevertheless, from a human perspective, I could not help but struggle to understand or appreciate what crime I had committed to warrant this level of battle. Notwithstanding, I was determined to win the battle regardless of my struggling human perception to understand what on earth I could have done to land me on this 'Armageddon' battlefront.

Aside from the terrible smell in the atmosphere, I realised my opponents were some countless ugly looking beings that seem very determined to destroy me. I heard many voices say "Welcome to hell You have no chance, just kill yourself or better still, do everyone a favour and kill someone". For several days, I was under heavy spiritual attack. I kept on praying and as I carried on praying, I continued to have all the right words to counteract my opponent's evil instructions that I should kill myself or go out and kill someone. After what seemed like many days on my feet, my legs felt as if they were ready to give up on me. They started to wobble yet I was unable to sit down or stop uttering the sporadic 'word' that was coming out of my mouth. I became so thirsty and felt like I was going to pass out. Although, on one hand I was feeling so physically weak, on the other hand I felt so strong and seemed to have an unexplainable energy from within me, which was enabling me to continue battling and remaining standing on my feet.

After what seemed like endless years in this battle, I felt I needed help. However, when I cried and shouted for help no one seemed to care. Instead, the ugly creatures made fun of me for trying to seek help. I had no idea of the time or day and even though I could see that I was still in this physical world, it was as if the clock had permanently stopped moving forward from the midnight hour and everything appeared to be upside down. As the battle intensified, hell started to unravel itself before my very eyes. I saw that hell is a realm of combined segments of regimental powers and the main agenda of each regiment is to permanently destroy human souls. Each regiment has a principality-head and each principality-head is a record keeper of a 'book of death'. One of the books was opened and I saw written in it, names of every creature under the regiment and records of their visits to earth. Written beside every name was: Time, Date and Place of Birth. Also included was the expected time place and cause of death to end their earthly journey. Some of the names had records of several visits while others only had a record of one visit.

While it was clearly apparent to me from what I was seeing,

that the objective of the entire hell-regiment is to lead human beings on earth to a self-destructive end, every hell-regiment seemed to have their own evil and wicked area of speciality. The entire game of the regiments of evil is to make everything that is detrimental to the human soul appear as a good thing to practice and live by. For instance, the special aim of the magic and witchcraft regiment is to convince people in the world that practicing magic and witchcraft is good, harmless fun. As the mysteries of hell continued to unfold before my very eyes, I clearly could see that the entire regiment of hell is into sexual domination of vulnerable human beings. To achieve their sexual domination aim, they inundate the world channel waves with lustful images and materials to entrap the mind, body and spirit in darkness, so that the enslaved human spirit can keep on fulfilling the lustful desires of the hell-regiments. Each regiment has uncountable ugly beings whose main task is to lead human beings into self-destruction.

Although the entire darkness regiments has as their common goal the destruction of human beings, I found that the different regiments were at constant loggerheads as a result of their personal interests to control the world territories. However, I soon realised that when it came to fulfilling their wicked insatiable desire to destroy me, they were all fully united amongst themselves and not at all at loggerheads. In their wicked hearts and minds of unity, they strategically worked together to wage their war of destruction against me.

As the battle progressed, I began to see that their common-unity warfare approach was something they considered necessary to maintain, so as to bombard me with relentless spiritual attacks from all angles in order to force me into a quick surrender. They had an endless line of regimental soldiers all readily positioned to attack me one after the other. The regiment at the starting line was the regiment of 'fear' and just as I was beginning to conclude that this regiment was the worst of all, I soon discovered that 'fear' was just the beginning of their spiritual weapons repertoire. From further revelations I began seeing the faces of the inhabitants of hell more clearly and I was able to recognise some of the faces as that of dead relatives. However, most shockingly, I was surprised to see several faces of the worldly famous both deceased and living still on earth, plenteously spread across the entire hell-regiments as the enslaved—subject to the ruling forces controlled by the powers of evil.

Whilst I was still struggling to digest my shocking revelations, I discovered that hell in its entire regimental force has an operative hierarchical system—a distinctive ruling order. At the top end of hell's hierarchical spiritual order are the fallen angels headed by Lucifer. The fallen angels act as hierarchal heads of the entire regiment of hell, and they have their subordinate 'divisional' territorial leaders. These subordinate territorial 'leaders' are spiritual warlords. As spiritual warlords, they are carefully positioned in the high places of the world for the sake of implementing hell's wicked destructive spiritual order in the global world. The territorial leaders and warlords have as their subordinates several territorial agents and legions of demonic soldiers that are readily loitering around in their divisional territories to obey their orders of destruction.

The demonic spirits work closely with the territorial agents to serve the overall wicked purpose of the leader of each division. The demonic forces of evil accomplish their divisional leader's destructive aims by the application of three main evil spiritual strategies. The first is to do with segmenting themselves into various kinds of spiritual stronghold blocks. Secondly, from these various stronghold blocks, they systematically come together to visibly erect a masquerading sinful order 'image'—a deceptive ploy to sugar coat and sanction sin. Thirdly, glamorisation of the sinful order for the sake of ring fencing the will of the unsuspecting humans within the controlling powers of the axes of evil. Once the image of sin becomes visibly erected, the divisional leaders then steps in to enforce the sinful order over the willing and unwilling divisional inhabitants through wider fear embedded self-righteous laws.

These subordinate leaders of hell as territorial division leaders—are rulers of the world. As rulers of the world and direct subordinates of the fallen angels, their overall world assignment is to globally erect the ugly image of sin—and not just in their divisional territories. To accomplish this aim, the division leaders have as their overall mandate a unity objective of all divisional operations for the sake of erecting a global sinful self-righteous World Order system.

"For men shall be lovers of their own selves, covetous, boasters, proud, blasphemers, disobedient to parents, unthankful, unholy, without natural affection, trucebreakers, false accusers, incontinent, fierce, despisers of those that are good, traitors, heady, high-minded, lovers of pleasures more than lovers of God having the form of godliness, but denying the power thereof: from such turn away".   —2 Timothy 3:2-5

I discovered as more revelations began to unfold that the realm of hell as a whole is made up of fire-layers. I saw that most of the so-called stars that are considered by the human population to be enjoying themselves on earth are actually at the hottest layer of hell fire, undergoing immense suffering. Through further revelations, I realised that the so-called world famous and stars occupy the worst places in hell as a reward for the important roles they have played in erecting the image of sin in the human world population. The primary goal of the division heads of evil is to continually engineer and conform unsuspecting human minds into desiring worldly things. They mainly achieve this aim through glamorising vanity as true riches in order to ensure that the human focus remains entirely worldly and from worldliness—dedication to sinfulness. To fulfil this evil objective, the divisional-heads of evil via their territorial agents recruited several dead spirits in the world to be their channels of evil. They afforded them worldly stardom status and tasked them to camouflage vanity as prosperity for the sake of corrupting the human minds across the globe with vanity desires.

As more revelations continued to unfurl, I noted that the appearance of every spirit in hell does not look like a normal earthly human. Instead, the spirits were very ugly looking and weird in nature. Though they were non-human looking in appearance, I recognised their world faces from a mirror-looking object that is directly in front of their faces. Not only are hell spirits ugly and weird looking, they also smell terribly and the smell was nothing like anything I have ever smelt on earth. Generally speaking, the entire picture of hell was the complete opposite to what the ordinary eyes sees in the world. I saw what the world considered as beautiful faces looking gruesome and ugly; the so- called rich looking pitifully ugly and wretched. Every hell creature including the regimental-heads is a spiritual criminal and as spiritual criminals they are enslaved in hell to serve time with hard labour. They all have huge steel looking objects tied to their feet and the steel was as huge as a house. Although they were all full of sorrow and clearly suffering immensely, they were unrepentant, mean looking and wickedly evil in their appearance.

From the moment I entered into the revelation 'arena', everyone in my immediate physical surroundings looked strange and began to act strangely. Everyone known and unknown to me became directly and indirectly against me and there seemed to be no end to the demonic regimental attacks toward me. Having undergone what seemed like timeless, relentless spiritual attacks—my physical body weakened. The weaker I got, the more I tried to remain mentally alert so that I could continue to counteract the attacks from the never ending different regiments with the only weapon I had—words. However, the more I saw of hell's secrets, the more intense my spiritual battle became. Deep within the heartland of my battles, I could hear the hell-regimental spirits repeatedly saying, "The Lamb is light and the world belongs to darkness, hence the truth must not plainly come out, so that darkness would continue to rule in the world".

Based upon their continuous affirmations, I recognised the primary reason for finding myself at the forefront of this spiritual battleground was as a result of God's calling upon my life, which is to witness across the world that Christ Jesus is the only Truth. Judging by the extreme viciousness of their attacks against me, it appeared the entire regimental forces of hell were determined to prevent me from my mission through their warfare efforts. They were determined to do anything and everything to prevent me from openly testifying and witnessing to the world that the Lamb of God, Jesus Christ is the entire Truth. As a result of their non-stop bombarding attacks against me, I became increasingly weaker and physically tired. My body felt battered and as I have I noted -- there were visible bruises all over my physical body.

Even though the suffering of the inhabitants of hell is immensely great, they didn't seem to care about their sufferings. They were wickedly desperate to do anything to prevent what they all agreed was the truth about Christ coming plainly out into the open. Every creature I saw looked beastly and many had heads like that of a wolf. Every regiment had uncountable ugly spirits and their main aim was to keep me forever locked-up in the land of death. The more I resisted one regiment with a counteractive word that now seemed to be flowing non-stop from within me, the fiercer the battle I faced in the next regiment. The regiments got increasingly fiercer and the longer the battle continued, the weaker I became, physically. I no longer had any idea how long I had been standing on my feet and I had not had any sleep since it all started. At any rate, I did not wish to fall asleep because I was afraid that once I closed my eyes, I would never wake-up again.

Regardless of my physically tiredness, I always had the right 'word' to say. The word or words that I spoke were my weaponry defence and I had plentiful armoury of words coming out of me beyond my human understanding. I was determined to win the battle and somehow, I felt I needed to go through what I was going through for the sake of entire 'life goodness'. I had an unexplainable confidence that I was going to win and although it seemed like God had abandoned me, something kept assuring me that He was behind the scenes steering me along.

The entire regiment of hell looked very filthy and the atmospheric realm smelt like millions of decomposed dead bodies. I felt choked by the smell and all I wanted was to escape from it back to normal life. However, the more I tried to free myself the more resistance I faced. No matter what I did or said, it seemed like the end was not in sight and the regiments seemed to be endless. Every time I thought that I had seen the last of the regiments, another one would appear with fiercer, ugly looking creatures. As the spiritual battle progressed from one regiment to another, my eyes became reacquainted with my normal visible surroundings.

I saw and realised that the wicked, ugly demonic creatures are everywhere in the visible world realm, hibernating in humans and destroying them from the inside. I saw many humans walking around in the company of uncountable demons and several were deeply engaged in conversations with them. Some were audible in their conversations, in what seemed to be conversations with themselves since no ordinary eyes could see their demonic companions, whilst others were busy engaged in silent conversations with the demons in their minds. The demons were busy abusing the humans calling them ugly, smelly and much more pouring non-stop abusive words into their minds. The human beings in the company of these demons were extremely depressed and sorrowful.

The more I saw hell for what it is, the more my visible surroundings started fading, and as it was gradually fading away, I started going in and out of consciousness. As I went in and out of consciousness, I began to see the world fully as a world that is full of dead demonic spirits of hell. The people around me in the visible realm could not help me because naturally, they had no idea of what I was going through. To the ordinary eyes, my actions and reactions were strange and nothing short of madness. However, even though I recognised this, I had no way of stopping what was going on in the spiritual or prevent what to the ordinary eyes is nothing less than a shocking and seemingly confused reactions to it. Worse still, I soon discovered as the battle progressed that no one on earth was on my side, for none helped me fight the battle. It seemed like all spirits of the world were now my battle opponents.

With no end in sight, I got to a point where I was in mind of giving up completely. But just as I was about to fade into complete unconsciousness, I heard a voice say: "The keys are in your hands, awake, open the gates and walk out". I looked and could not see any keys in my hands. However, the words that I heard gave me some renewed strength. In my renewed strength, I tried to walk out of the hellish realm and it seemed like my efforts were paying off, because I started coming back to consciousness.

But, just as I was about to celebrate my consciousness and possibly freedom from hell, I heard for the first time, a voice that introduced himself as Satan, say: "You simply cannot leave just like that. You are a sinner and as a sinner, you are of flesh. As flesh, you are in covenant of sin to die forever and those who are in covenant to die must remain in death".

The voice that said I had the keys responded by saying, "This covenant is broken by the blood of the Lamb". Directing His statement back to me, the voice said, "Fear not, this is so that you may know that salvation from hell is not by your might or power but by the power of the Holy Ghost. So, now arise Daughter of Zion and move in the goodness light of the Father, Son and the Holy Spirit".

I immediately tried to arise and move as He said. However, I discovered that my legs were so heavy and my body had become very stiff. I looked around, but there was no one to help me move my legs. The other spirits around me in chains started laughing wickedly at me and mocked me for even trying to get out. I beckoned them to help me escape so I that I can also help them gain their own freedom from the sorrowful hell-prison, but their response to me was in the form of more laughter. The more I sought their help, the more they showed me the steel on their feet and the chains around their legs. The more they drew my attention to their chains and heavy steel, the more they mocked me for trying to escape. Instead of helping, they desperately sought to compress me with every little movement they could make toward me. It then dawned on me that I was amongst extremely dangerous enemies who would stop at nothing in their attempt to destroy me. This made me feel so helpless and frustrated about everything that was happening to me. I was of the mind that the voice I heard telling me about the keys was that of Jesus, but He seemed to have gone again and left me to the misery of hell. I looked around me and realised that no one visible or invisible was friendly toward me and I felt completely alone. Whilst I was still busy trying to figure out a means of escape, the hell creatures suddenly started chanting:

We want power too and this power that we want is the power of the Lion of Judah! The secret of life is in the Lion of Judah. The power of the Lion of Judah is the power of creation and resurrection from death, and we know it is in you and you cannot proclaim that power because we will not let you. If you proclaim the good Name of the Lion of Judah in mystery Babylon, then mystery Babylon secret will be out in the Babylonian world, therefore we cannot let you escape to reveal our secrets.

As they were chanting, I continuously went in and out of consciousness and just as I thought I was about to lose total consciousness never to regain it, I heard the voice; which I believed to be that of Christ again say:

She is already in full victory. However, so that she knows she has total victory in all realms, the battle will now begin. False fear is the weapon of darkness. I have given her real power and with real power, she is no longer afraid of death. Being the only One that has entire universal power to save and destroy, I have marked her for My goodness and as the battle now fully begins, I decree that the goodness in her will prevail.

Immediately He finished speaking, I found myself in the midst of a spiritual battlefront beyond explanation and soon discovered that the battle that I thought I had seen before was simply preparation for the main war that I was now engaged in. The attacks came from every regimental angle. Nevertheless, the more intense the battle got, the more I waxed stronger in unexplainable strength. The attacks hurled against me by the regiments came raining in faster than ever before. It was as if they were now just raging past with heavy attacks, instead of staying to fight like before. I had more physical marks and bruises all over my body, but despite the intensity of their attacks on me, I remained fully standing, on my feet. In the regiment of diseases, I started to visibly foam in my mouth with all kinds of disease demons throwing disease darts at me. I heard voices say, "We have all kinds of diseases, take and foam in your mouth". Nonetheless, even though I was foaming in the mouth physically, I felt very strong spiritually and totally well, and I noted that the defensive 'word' of armoury coming out of me was causing serious damage to my already damaged opponents.

The countless demons from the different regimental forces kept on coming and there seemed to be no end in sight to these demonic regiments. However, as I carried on tackling them with my mysterious words of attacks and defence, I remained strong enough to carry on battling. Some of the words that were coming out of my mouth were so mysterious that I did not know their meanings. However, I was not so much concerned that I had no conscious physical understanding of these words because as far as I was concerned, they were effectively doing the defence and attack job.

Through revelations from God at a later stage, I learnt that the word that I was uttering was the powerful Word of redemption glory. This redemption Word of power is the defence and attacking spiritual sword and it is the Lion of Judah's Word—which is Christ, the oracle of life. This oracle Word of life is above all power and all authority in all realms and it is only with the Lion of Judah's 'sword' Word that any man can prevail over death in the land of the living dead.

The creatures of hell seemed bent on remaining in their hellish prison. Several times in the midst of this battle, I cried and wept bitterly, both for what I was going through and for what I was now able to see people going through in the invisible reality world of hell. As my warfare experience progressively worsened, I had at some point stopped pacing around and ended up physically standing at the same spot for a period that seemed like years on end. Having been on my feet at the same spot for what appeared to be an endless duration, I had gotten to a point whereby my legs had gone completely stiff and my eyes were burning red—full of grief and pain. My entire body felt as if compressed with some huge heavy still and no matter how hard I tried, I found it impossible to move from the spot that I ended up standing in. I felt entirely stiffened with extreme fear and grief and all I wanted was a complete end to the battle that I had suddenly found myself engaged in.

The demonic soldiers of hell seemed determined to destroy me at all cost and instead of surrendering, they kept on saying, "All we have to give you is sickness and pain". Even though I had been all along feeling strong and unyielding to their attacks, I increasingly became weaker, physically. My physical body didn't seem to be holding strongly to their non-stop bombardment. Worse of all, the bruises on my physical body had gotten to an unbearable level whereby I felt I could not take anymore. From facing their non-stop attacks, I reached a stage where I got tired of counteracting their attacks and simply gave up. In giving up, I found myself in a place darker than what I had seen so far. After some period of blankness in this darker place, I became once again conscious to my entire visible world surroundings. I found that every creature I was now seeing looked worse than the ones I had seen before.

I saw beings of different kinds of shapes and sizes walking around everywhere. Some of them had heads and tails like that of the wolf animal. Some had three heads with one eye in the middle of their forehead. I heard animals especially dogs barking non-stop and I understood that it was because of what they could see, that mankind cannot see with their ordinary eyes. The terrible smell in the earth's atmosphere in this darker place went from bad to worse and the evil pictures of hell became even more clearly visible to me—more than ever before. It was as if hell was all along invisibly in the world, and had now surfaced from the invisible to visible surface.

With the invisible picture of hell on earth now entirely visible for me to see, I was able to see even more clearly the hellish uncountable deadly demonic predators prowling everywhere in the world hungrily seeking after the human flesh to devour. From all I was now seeing, I became even more afraid and I wanted nothing to do with the world because no part of it seemed a safe place. My entire body ached physically. I was weak and thirsty and at this point I felt completely dead. I saw a very thick darkness covering everywhere. However, in the midst of this thick darkness, my eyes opened to see from afar what looked like a flash of light. With all the energy and determination I had left in me, I crawled toward this light. What I found when I reached where the light was coming from—was an extraordinary beautiful place.

CHAPTER THREE
HEAVEN REVEALED

"And immediately I was in the Spirit: and, behold, a throne was set in heaven, and one sat on the throne. And he that sat was to look upon like a jasper and a sardine stone: and there was a rainbow round about the throne, in sight like unto an emerald".

—Revelation 4:2-3

When I reached where the light was coming from, I found myself in a place that looked beautiful beyond comprehension. I heard a voice say:

The wish of the wicked is to remain wicked and in their wickedness, have beauty as a reward. The wish of the wicked is for the good at heart to be in hell and for the wicked to be in heaven. The world is the opposite of the real world. The wicked see themselves in a fake-heaven and they tempt the good at heart to make the world believe that goodness only attracts pain and suffering.

Although I could hear the voice, I did not see the face of the speaker. However, from hearing this voice, I became full of strength, and in greater renewed strength, I felt fully energized, strong and ready to carry on. I continued admiring the beauty of the place that I found myself in and the more I looked, the more I kept saying to myself, "This is too beautiful and no wicked-minded being must ever enter this place".

With those words repeatedly playing in my mind, I noted that my surroundings were covered with rays of powerful shining lights. The beauty of the place was quite overwhelming and I kept thinking that I must defend the place so that no wicked-minded being would ever be able to come in and destroy it. I thought to myself, "Surely this must be the land of entire universal beauty and if the wicked of the world were to discover it, they would try to destroy it with their evil, which would mean there would be no beauty or goodness left in the entire universe".

Whilst I was still busy trying to figure out how to defend the place, I noted that there were many 'shining beings' around me, smiling at me and very friendly toward me. They were all looking joyful and powerfully natured. From where I was, I could see surrounding streets paved with many precious stones and sidewalks flowing with rivers made of light. I also saw many fountains made with fire and I could hear beautiful songs of praise coming from everywhere. I could hear the beautiful beings singing:

> The Lord of Hosts sits upon His Throne and all the angels and saints sing His praises. His presence is full of amazing beauty. His palace is with many rooms and the many rooms are full of many treasures. His children are gods and they wear a crown of many precious stones that sparkle like fire. His garment is made of fire and His crown is like a million sparkling stars.

As I continued to take in the beauty of my surroundings, I

realised the place I was in is some gigantic, amazing looking courtyard compared to nothing on earth. The flooring was made with bright shining stones and I noted there were many powerful and beautiful looking creatures everywhere. I tried to speak to some of the creatures, but each time I tried to open my mouth to speak, words would simply fail me because I was too overwhelmed with the beauty of the place. As I continued to look around, I saw even more beautiful beings, this time around, riding on beautiful horses that had wings. The horse riders were each carrying staffs in their hands, and on their backs they had what looked like golden water spraying containers. They all wore shining helmets of fire on their heads, and their eyes sparkled like stars. They had bright-shining light sandals on their feet and their beauty is beyond description. Their clothing was like some armoured garment and it was as if it is made of fire They were quite many in number, and as they continued to ride past, they were looking my way and smiling. I then heard one say, "We are the warriors of heaven and we are of the Holy Ghost. Do not be afraid".

Deep in total fascination of everything that was happening around me, I suddenly became aware of and saw a being that seemed to have been standing right beside me all along. He had a bright shining, light body and huge beautiful fiery wings and his eyes sparkled like fire. His head was like that of a man but his beauty was beyond description. He was mightily tall and breathtakingly handsome. I was so overwhelmed with his beauty and with everything else that I was seeing, and felt I should say something. But every time I tried to speak, I was unable to. It was as if he had wanted me to fully digest the beauty of my surroundings before noticing him. As soon as I noticed that he had been standing next to me, he smiled and

said, "You have sought and you have found. Now I will give you a tour, so that you will know that Zion is real. The Lord has asked me to do this and I am Gabriel, the bearer of Good News".
I wanted to comment on his wondrous beauty, but I still could not say a word. He then said, "Do not be afraid, follow me for you have found grace before the Lord and blessed are you in the House of the Lord, now and forever". When he said, 'follow me', I immediately saw us standing on a mountaintop and from that location I could see my immediate and far off surroundings a lot clearer than before. He looked toward me and said, "The Kingdom of God is for the faithful and righteous. This that you see is the inheritance for the saints at heart". As he was speaking, I kept my eyes fixed on what he was showing me and no matter how hard I tried to say something, no word came out.

As I continued gazing admiringly at everything, he asked, "What do you see"? It was as if all I had needed to be able to speak was to hear this question from him. I opened my mouth and started to tell him everything I was seeing. I started by saying:

What I am seeing is beyond beautiful. I can see beautiful beings everywhere. They have beautiful crowns on their heads and these crowns are made of many precious stones that sparkle like fire. I see roads paved with many precious stones that are shining like bright lights and I see many things that are too beautiful to describe. I see a river and this river has four adjoining heads. I see a mountain made of salt. I see many horses with wings flying all around and I see many creatures that are mysterious to look at, but breathtakingly beautiful. I see a temple of light and in front of this temple, there are many angelic looking beings standing at guard and singing. I see a river of life and sidewalks lit with beautiful rays of light. I see a beautiful tree guarded by beautiful beings armed with long two-edged swords made of shimmering lights of flaming fire, brandishing their swords from time to time. I see the tree has light looking fruits and everywhere is full of bright-shining lights. I see many beautiful beings wearing crowns of light on their heads with 'Holiness Unto the Lord' written on them. I see a place that seems to be the source of many treasures. All the creatures that I see in this place have in their possession many of these treasures. They play with them as if they are some sort of toy and no one seems to care about it so much because it is available everywhere.

Whilst I was telling the angel who had introduced himself as Gabriel the things I was seeing, the mountaintop we were standing on started to shake and I became really afraid. The Angel said, "Fear not for the Lord comes in His chariot of glory unto this Holy Mountain and as He comes the heavens and the earth shake". Immediately, as he finished saying these words I saw someone riding on a chariot made of many bright fiery lights coming toward us. His beauty was greater than all that I had seen so far. As He got closer to where we were, I bowed down and said, "Please have mercy upon me, O Great One".

The angel beside me was also head bowed and I was shaking with fear. He walked toward us and said, "Fear not for you have found grace before Me". His voice was like thundering rain but it was gentle and soft to my ears. He said, "I am the Christ who died, resurrected, and lives forever, follow me". As soon as He said, 'follow me' I found myself in another place more beautiful than all the places that I had seen so far. I noticed that there were seven giant light candles placed on something that looked like a golden tray around the hallway and the candles never seemed to burn out.

I saw many instruments of praise hanging on the wall playing on their own and the music was sweet and of good melody. I saw a gigantic throne and on the throne was another who looked just like Christ. The One sitting on the throne had a similar garment to Christ's and the garment had many bright looking precious stones. The stones that the garment was made of sparkled of fire and the fire that was emanating from it resembled star-looking objects and they were dropping everywhere. I prostrated before the throne and was too afraid to say anything. I then heard the voice of Christ say, 'Look up'. When I looked up, I saw that Christ and the One on the throne were actually: One. I noticed that I was now alone in a huge hall with the One on the throne. When He started speaking, the whole place began to shake and His voice sounded like thundering rain. He began by saying:

> Welcome and do not be afraid for you have found grace. Fear not and be of good courage, for I am with you always. Write these things down that I am about to tell you and tell it to the world as a testimony of Truth. Let those that have ears, hear.

As soon as He said, 'Let those that have ears, hear', a writing pen and a large scroll appeared in my hands. As He continued to speak, it was as if my hand was now operating with its own mind. My hands started to jot down everything He was saying with such high speed. I seemed to have no control whatsoever over the writing operations my hands started to perform.

God's Word of Testimony

I am the Father, the Son and the Holy Ghost. The only One God who was, who is and who ever shall be. I am the Creator of the universe and I am love. Everything you see is invisible to man and it is only the good on deeds that shall inherit the goodness of My Kingdom. Do not be afraid for all is well that ends well. You have sought and you have found. You have knocked and the door is wide open for you. You have asked and the answer is given to you. You have followed the narrow road and you have found the goodness of light. Heaven is a land of glory and the glory of heaven is the goodness of love. Only the loving-hearted shall inherit the new earth and only those whose hands and feet are clean shall eat and dine with the elders of heaven. The elders of heaven shall not dine with the filthy and unclean beast. Only the saints shall see My light. The demonic beings shall be in the dark and in the darkness of their soul—they shall be full of fear.

I opened your eyes to see what is invisible to humans and I opened your ears to make you hear My voice. This is My commandment to you, do all that I say is right for only I know what is right and wrong. The world hates My righteousness for humans are desperately evil and wicked. The world hates love—for in sin man is full of hatred. The world hates goodness, because evil is in the hearts of humans and the evil of humans oppresses their souls in death due to their persistent evil ways in the world. Wickedness is the aim and desire of humans in the world. As slaves of evil, they are only in mind to serve the evil demonic purposes of their dead masters. The wicked tries the righteous in the world, for humans in the world are only mindful of pursuing self-righteousness.

The righteous are not afraid of trials, for they know within their souls that eternal goodness awaits them. The wicked and evil-minded see themselves as having fun in the world. They dance around thinking they are winners, not knowing that they are mad and their dance is of sorrow and madness. To have a mind of wickedness and expect rewards of goodness is evidence of madness.

The trial of a saint is to perfect the soul, but the wicked will perish in their sorrow that they consider as enjoyment. No human shall see the light of glory unless in heart of goodness. No human shall inherit the new heaven and earth, unless they are in heart of loving-kindness. No human of the carnal flesh shall enter the gates of My kingdom, for My kingdom is for the good on deeds. All that you see, no humans can see with their ordinary eyes, and all that I show you, is so that you will know there is justice beyond the world and My justice is total and complete justice.

Do not be afraid of the world, for the earth is My footstool. With Me, you are more than a conqueror and no weapon fashioned or formed against you shall prosper. The world tries the saints for their submitting to My righteousness. The flesh hates My divine love, for My divine love is perfect sacrificial love and all that humans are interested in is to be abominable meat to the devil. The flesh loves to sin and the will of humans in sin is of extreme wickedness. They slaughter themselves daily as meat for the beast and they perish for they seek with a carnal mind. Those who walk in the flesh as flesh are slaves unto sin, but those who walk in the Spirit are in Me. I AM that I AM, Master in all dominion. I am all power and as the All Powerful God, I am above all principalities and powers. Your trials shall be many but your reward shall be exceedingly great and plenteous, for whosoever is of goodness shall never lack in profit of goodness.

The whoremongers shall perish and the evil hearted will perish in their own evil. The Truth is I, and I—the Trinity One God is the everlasting, great: I AM THAT I AM. Those who know the Father, the Son and the Holy Spirit shall have the keys to unlock mysteries. However, those who bow their heads to the beast shall perish forever in their soul. I AM the God of gods, I know those that worship Me and they know Me. My sheep know Me as their Shepherd, hence David said: "The Lord is my Shepherd and I shall not want". Those who call on Me and know Me are alive in their soul. Those who persevere in their trials and tribulations shall have triumphant joy always, and in triumphant joy they shall be solid as a rock in Me, the Rock of all ages. Those who believe in the Son believe in I, the Father and only through My only begotten Son shall any spirit be a son of Mine. The Truth is Christ and no man can have salvation without Christ.

Any man that follows the path of principalities shall condemn his or her soul to eternal hell damnation. To have the Truth is to be in light. To believe in a liar is to remain in darkness of the evil dead. The evil dead is carnally minded and to be Carnal is to operate in a mind of illusion. Carnality enslaves humans in deep illusions and no human shall come out of these deadly illusions without Christ. Christ is My light revealed, and any man that rejects Christ rejects the light. Light is the ruling power of the universe and darkness cannot prevail over light. Anyone that is in My light is in My presence, and in My presence they shall be partakers of My everlasting dominion, power and authority. Only in Christ shall a person be in vision of heaven, and in vision of heaven, be in goodness hope of eternal life and peace. Christ is heaven revealed and if Christ is in your heart, you are at the heart of heavenly glory. This is the wisdom of life and this is the Truth and the whole truth.

Go into the world and spread the Gospel news to the ends of the earth, and just as I promised you, I will be with you now and in eternity. Declare the Truth with boldness and do not be afraid of the devilish spirits of the world, for they are prisoners of darkness and all their evil shall only work to your advantage. Hold on to the Word of faith and remember all that you see now is your inheritance now and forever. Go and speak the Truth. If man condemns you for speaking the Truth, know that I have justified you in the blood of the Lamb. Go and warn the nations that it is time to repent, for judgment is at hand. Proclaim to the world that the Kingdom of Heaven is real and My desire for humans is for their souls to be free from hell.

Tell the nations to repent for it shall be too late to plead for mercy and grace when Judgement Day arrives. Go and the whole of heaven shall go with you. Do not fear the world for there is nothing in the world but false fear. Do not be afraid of death for I have abolished death for you by My perfect and loving sacrifice. Let those that have ears hear the Word of true faith. Those who fail to listen and continue to feed their sinful and lustful flesh with more sin shall die and never shall they rise again. The righteous that dies as flesh shall rise again, for I shall raise him/her up to dwell in My heavenly abode everlastingly. A righteous one shall not perish in death for to be righteous is to be light, and darkness can never prevail over light.

I am the God of the universe and My Name is YAHWEH. My spoken Word of faith is Christ and between Christ and Myself, there is no difference. Let those who are in mind of divine and loving sacrifice continue their walk in perfect mind of goodness for their reward shall be without an end. They shall dwell in My presence forever and have eternal peace and rest in My dominion of power now and forever more. Say to the nations I AM that I AM is love. If any humans seek Me with a repentant heart they shall find me. However, the liars and pretenders shall continue to deceive themselves and shall never find My Truth. They will continue to be slaves unto Satan and just like their wicked master, they shall perish in the lake of fire that burns forever.

The true Gospel is the Gospel of Resurrection. Go now in peace and proclaim the Gospel of resurrection, which is the Gospel of victory in all revelation. Fear not for I am always by your side, to take you to the finishing line of your mission.

Go in joy and in peace, and know that I will never leave nor forsake you. As I was with the saints before you, so will I be with you now and forever. Be not afraid of the wicked. The wicked are full of fear and all they desire is to sell their fear to others in order to cripple them. The true Word of faith is in you and no one can silence the Truth. Christ is Word, as Word righteousness and as righteousness, the ONLY TRUE POWER that is above all powers and principalities. I created all things with My Word and My perfect Word of creation is Christ.

All those that are in Christ are perfect in Me, but those that are without Christ are void of life and of the real power of life. Those that try to silence the Word of faith shall not see the light of day. They shall remain in the domain of darkness for their wickedness, and because they are darkness hearted, they shall perish in their souls everlastingly. Be of good courage always and be full of joy, knowing that heaven is in you and you are in reward of heaven, for you have found grace before Me. Peace be unto you and blessed are those that seek goodness in their heart for you. Be of a good cheer always for as My Chosen, My goodness and mercies shall follow you all the days of your life.

Woe unto the evil hearted for they are abominable meat of the beast. This is wisdom; let those that have ears, hear the Word of wisdom for the goodness sake of their souls. This is the true Word of life and My Word of life is living water in the soul. Those that have My living water in their soul shall never thirst for they shall be in goodness fulfilment. This is My Word of spiritual sight and vision from I, The—I AM, the

Host of heaven, the everlasting King in all dominion and dimensional realms. No one without My revelation can have vision of heaven on earth. Heaven is My domain and unless I open the eyes to see, no man can see Zion, My Holy City. I am the only one that can open and shut the eyes. So that you have perfect knowledge of the whole Truth to give as testimony to mankind in the end of days, I have in this day opened your eyes to see and hear these things. Zion is real and this is My Word to mankind, let those that have ears, hear. Let those that hear, repent from their evil and wicked ways, for the Day of Judgement is at hand.

My Ark of Covenant is Christ and once I shut the door of the Ark, no one shall be able to enter again. Repent! O ye humans in mystery Babylon. The fire is raging in mystery Babylonia and those that bow their heads to the image of the beast shall be meat to the beast. Evil shall face the wicked, and the wicked shall perish in his own wickedness in eternal damnation of death. Let the wise seek wisdom from life. Let them follow Christ and not perish but have an everlasting life of peace, joy, and rest. For only Christ can lead the soul to My presence. Those that are without Christ shall not enter My Holy Mountain to be in My presence. Those that cannot enter cannot share from My treasure chest and proceeds of My Holy Mountain. Those that are without Christ shall not see the goodness of My face, for Christ is the goodness of My face revealed and to reject Christ is to choose My wrath.

Christ is the Lamb that took the blame of sin for the whole of mankind and those in Christ shall no longer be blamed or condemned for their sins. Christ is returning soon and anybody that He finds in sin shall carry their sinful blame on their own head forever. These things I have shown you, so that humans will have it as a true testimony from now until the end of days. Speak the Truth always, for woe to liars and woe to the evil and the wicked. I have called you in order to send you to the nations, and you will speak My Word to the nations as I have sent you. Woe unto those that I have not sent and who claim that I have sent them. Go in peace and all that is of power and might go with you. My grace shall remain with you now and forevermore. Fear no more for your battle is over and victory is yours in Me now and forevermore. Your trials are over, for in this day and forever you shall have exceedingly great reward in Me, for you have found grace. The world is full of illusion and the illusion of the world is what the wicked see as reality. I have shown you these things for you to have perfect knowledge of reality. Now rejoice, celebrate, and fear not the world, for I Christ have already conquered the world for you.

As soon as He finished saying these words, my hands automatically stopped writing and the pen and scroll, which were like nothing on earth both disappeared straight into my heart. I tried to say something but nothing came out. Whilst I was still pondering on what to say, I found myself in a place that looked like an assembly hall filled with many instruments of praise. The place that we were before was relatively small, compared to where I now found myself. The size of the hall was twice the size of the earth and it was full of all kinds of beautiful beings. The place looked like an assembly hall for celebrations and it seemed all had gathered for a special celebration. The many beautiful creatures engaged in powerful songs and dance and everyone looked joyful beyond description. I noticed that the place was full of powerful lightings and the lighting in the place was brighter than the sun. The light had a spectrum of colours it illuminated as the beautiful creatures sang and danced. The songs were very soothing and they brought so much joy and gladness to my heart.

The beauty of the place was incredibly breathtaking and the more I looked the more I kept thinking: "I am certainly not leaving this place ever again". I looked and saw a throne twice as huge as the one I had seen before. Sitting on the throne was the Great I AM; only now He looked more powerful, brighter and more beautiful beyond what I can describe. The throne like the one before was made with stones that are too beautiful and precious to describe. His garment was like some ceremonial garment, shinier and even more sparkling. He wore a crown made of many precious stones that looked like stars and they sparkled so brightly and seemed to be turning round like fiery lights on His head. His appearance was like that of many bright lights. He had a shining face and an illuminating body that is like millions of florescent lights.

All the beautiful-beings in the hall bowed their heads to worship the Great I AM who was on the Throne. They danced to powerful worship songs and their dance seems like some form of power demonstration. Everyone looked joyful beyond description and the more they worshiped and danced, the more they glowed and shined in their appearance. Their worship songs were highly moving and the more I watched what was going on, the more I kept saying to myself, "I am definitely not leaving this place ever again". The more they sang, the greater the light they received from the Throne and the greater the light they received from the Throne, the brighter the place got.

Earth is a relatively ugly place compared to the beauty of what I was seeing. The assembly hall looked so clean and the songs were very moving, so much so that I desperately wanted to join in. However, each time I tried to open my mouth to join in on the singing, I felt like crying instead. Deep into my fascination of the beauty of heaven, I suddenly became aware there was another beautiful being now standing by my side. The moment I became aware of him standing by my side, he introduced himself to me as Michael, the victorious archangel and with a gentle but firm tone of voice then said, "There are no tears allowed in this place. This is the land of victory and joy and no tears are allowed". He was breathtakingly handsome, but fiercer looking than all the other beings that were in the presence of the Great I AM in the assembly hall.

Since I was unable to join in because I could not help myself from wanting to cry, I decided it was best to heed to the gentle warnings of the Archangel Michael and remain a silent onlooker. I watched the beautiful light-looking beings worship in fullness of joy before the Throne of The I AM and the more they sang and worshiped, the more the Great I AM from His Throne gave them His light power. As they received power, they became so full of His power. Filled with so much of His power, they all in one voice and accord said:

Father we love You, Son we love You and Holy Spirit we love You. You are One in Your Holy Trinity and Holy is Your Name forever. You are the Great I AM and we shall worship

You, forever.

As I continued to be mesmerised by everything going on around me, the Archangel Michael who all along remained standing beside me smiled at me and said, "Now it is your turn to receive light- power"! Before I could ask anything, I heard a loud trumpet sound and straight after the trumpet sounded; one of the beautiful creatures spoke with a loud voice and said: Silence! For the Great One speaks. The Great I AM speaks. Let there be silence in the Tabernacle of His Holiness for the Lord speaks. Let all hear.

Immediately after the announcement, there was total silence and I suddenly found myself on my knees with my head fully bowed before the Throne of the Great I AM. When He started to speak, the entire place shook at the tone of His voice and I was greatly afraid. I was even more afraid than before, when He looked toward me with His shining beautiful face and said:

Welcome O daughter of Zion to the assembly of the heavenly saints. You still have to return to the Earth and complete your mission and everything you need is in your hands. The reward of Good News is on your side and total victory is standing by you. You have nothing to fear. Look in your hands and tell me what can you see.

I looked in my hands and unlike before, I now saw a staff and a key, so I answered: 'A staff and a key'. He then said:

The Staff is the authority you require to use the key. The key is what you need to open the door and walk out of the darkness realm you previously found yourself in. To start your great mission in the world, you must face death and bind death. You have victory over death because I have already abolished death for you. However, so that you know that death has no power over you, I have allowed you to face and bind death, in order to esteem you in My perfect holiness and glory. The key is mine, and I am the Master key holder. I have dipped the key in your hand in the blood of the Holy Lamb. You had the key and the staff in your hand all along so why have you not used it to open the door?

I answered, "It is because I am afraid and besides, when I looked in my hands before I found nothing there".

He replied, "The key and staff were there all along and the reason why you were not able to see them is because you were afraid. So what is the cause of your fear"?

I answered by saying, "I am afraid of death and because I am afraid of death, I cannot face death".

The Great I AM then said:

Because you are afraid of death, you have already died, but your soul is already saved by Me. So though you have died because you were afraid, you are also still alive. Although you are dead in your flesh, you are alive in your spirit and all you have to do to be back in full life consciousness is give fear to death in all realms. Once you give fear to death in all realms, you will clearly see that you are in full resurrection of life and that you already have victory over death in all dominion dimensional realms. You shall see the liar beast in his true evil and darkness colour.

However, know that the beast you see is not above you. He has already fallen down flat and cannot withstand you, for I have destroyed him so he has no power over you. It is so that you know that he has fallen, that I brought him out of his hiding to reveal him to you. If your enemy that was once invisible is now visible to you, then know that you have every power over that enemy and as such, he no longer has any real opposition power against you. It is for you to be certain of your victory that you go through this battle. You already have victory because there is no longer condemnation for you since you are in the Son, and in the Son you are now and forever fully in Me.

Therefore do not be afraid at all, for all you have to do, as I have said, is give the false fear of death unto death and march on in your victory in joy of eternal life. There is nothing to fear but fear itself. In this day, I have pronounced fear on death and death is afraid of you, because even though you have met death face to face, you are still alive. Death no longer has power over your soul. So go now, give fear of death unto death and let the devil rot in his shame in eternal death, for I am with you. All things now and forever shall certainly work together for your advantage and for your goodness, so do not be afraid for I am with you always.

With my head still bowed and with a shaky voice, I thanked the Great One. Although I was deeply afraid, I managed to ask, "How could I give fear to death"? The Great One answered:

By simply saying the Word and by the Word of authority, you give the fear of death back to death. The Word is in you and as you say the Word, so it shall be. I am the Oracle Word and the Word is in you, flowing like rivers of life. You belong to life and not death, and those who are alive in Me, death cannot keep down. By grace, I have saved you and by grace, I have given you the key in your hand. The battle that you face is not your battle but Mine. This battle is not unto death, for it is a battle that you must engage in, and see that you have won, in order to be fully certain that darkness has no power over you whatsoever.

It is a battle of life's revelations and it is not for you to die in it, but for you to see the strength that is in you from your eternal life existence in Me. Your soul is already in eternal life and your name will remain in My Book of Life. Since your name is in the Book of Life, it means you have everlasting victory over death. Therefore, arise and face this false fear with confidence of certainty, that you already have victory over death and know that I am with you always, now and forevermore. The battle appears fierce but victory is already yours and if you do all that I say is right, then you will see that death is already defeated. Now, go face your fear in total confidence of victory for I have already conquered death for you.

As He finished saying these words, there was so much light-force coming from Him and this light was so bright that all I could now see was light equivalent to a billion light volts. As this light filled the place, I started shaking all over and when I opened my mouth to speak, all I saw coming out was a 'sword of fire'. The whole assembly that was to this point very silent now went into some jubilant praise, displaying all kinds of powerful dance moves and several of them were spinning with so much speed in the air. With so much singing and dancing going on, the whole place became extremely brighter and more beautiful than it was beforehand. I kept thinking in my mind: "I cannot leave this beautiful place and go back to that ugly earth". With this thought going on in mind repeatedly, I felt I needed to plead with the Great I AM, so that He would not send me back to earth. Each time I tried to speak, the 'sword of fire' was all that came out of my mouth. It was as if talking time was over and everyone in the assembly seemed to only be interested in joyous celebration.

With everyone deep into this jubilation, I saw coming from the throne, highly powerful illuminating lights constantly changing from one beautiful colour of bright lights to another. I kept thinking I cannot leave this place and I desperately wanted to speak to the Great I AM, to plead with Him not to send me back to the world. However, each time I tried to say something all that kept coming from my mouth was the 'sword of fire'. I focused my eyes on the throne, hoping to see the reassuring smiling face of the, I AM again—so I could plead with Him not to send me back. Instead of His defined light shape, all I could now see coming from the throne were powerful light beams with no definable shape. With my eyes desperately fixed on the throne, I saw the defined smiling shining face of The I AM appear from the throne, now brighter than ever before and shining directly on me. All the while I was on my knees. However, when I saw His face shine on me once more, brighter than ever; my mind was at peace, full of His restful assurance. I prostrated fully in awe of His Holy and Majestic, glorious beauty and I was filled with so much gladness in my heart.

For the first time since I found myself in that glorious place, I felt very much at home and desperately wanted to be part of the joyous celebration that was going on around me. However, just as I was deliberating how best to participate in the major celebrations happening around me, I suddenly found myself in a place even much darker than I had been in before my awesome encounter with of the Great I AM.

All the beauty simply disappeared from my sight and I could see that I was now in the midst of the meanest—ugliest and most-wicked looking creatures imaginable—again. They all looked so mean and hungry and seemed ready to hastily devour me. I looked around and immediately realised I was back in hell.

CHAPTER FOUR
BACK IN HELL

"The sorrows of death compassed me, and the floods of ungodly men made me afraid. The sorrows of hell compassed me about: the snares of death prevented me. In my distress I called upon the LORD, and cried unto my God: he heard my voice out of his temple, and my cry came before him, even into his ears. Then the earth shook and trembled; the foundations also of the hills moved and were shaken, because he was wroth. There went up a smoke out of his nostrils, and fire out of his mouth devoured: coals were kindled by it. He bowed the heavens also, and came down: and darkness was under his feet. And he rode upon a cherub, and did fly: yea, he did fly upon the wings of the wind".

—Psalm 18: 4-10

Immediately, I found myself in a deep dark place, in the midst of the many ugly creatures that appeared hastily, ready to devour me. I heard a voice say:

The Power [Christ] is not in you so do not deceive yourself. You are dead and in death, you shall remain dead. Evil has total power and control and those who are on evil's side shall rule the universe. If you are good at heart, then you cannot have any peace, because this is my world and only the evildoers shall prosper.

I opened my mouth and said, "Satan you have fallen forever and I have victory over you everlasting".

71

The voice responded by saying, "If you have victory, then why are you here? Look at yourself and see your ugliness. How could power be in you when you are lying down dead? Try to rise and see if you can". I tried to rise and I couldn't. 'Look around you', he said, "And see my world. How do you think goodness or honesty can save you in this world"? After he finished saying this, I was able to see the full picture of the world again and I could see that the world is full of even more demonic spirits that are desperately evil. I could hear their voices coming from every corner of the world. I heard them say:

> We will fight you to the finish line. We will not allow you to bear witness or record to the goodness of the Lamb of God. It is true that the Word is God. It is also true that God through the Lamb gave mankind in the world, grace to be in His righteousness and in righteousness, to dwell in His holiness eternally if they repent from sin. However, we do not want any man to know that this is the Truth, therefore we will pollute the world with lies to confuse man so that man is not able to see the Truth.

Suddenly the face of the voice that asked, "If you have victory, why are you here?" became revealed to me. In the entire hell-regiment, he—Satan was the ugliest-looking being. He became even more ugly as he continued to speak and the uglier he got the more sorrowful he appeared to be.

Satan's Wicked Plan Revealed

Satan continued to reveal his wicked-plans by saying:

The world is already in confusion and we want it that way. Why should anyone have peace in my world when I have no peace or rest? My agents will silence and destroy anyone that wishes to bear witness or record of goodness in the world. We are your fear, you are sinners and as sinners, you belong to death. You have made a covenant with death and now you cannot escape. The world is a world of sin and fear and death must rule the world forever. My agents will deceive all and destroy many by leading their minds to be in confusion to die forever. People in the world shall not have a mind of awakening because I have corrupted their minds to addictively pursue vanity and have polluted their hearts to passionately desire and engage only in illicit sexual practices.

They will spend their time, busy trying to satisfy their illicit sexual urges and they shall have no control over it. Their minds shall work against them and sorrow will be great in their hearts. They will be full of extreme wickedness in their hearts and only be in mind to pursue money. In their love for money, they shall destroy one another and because of their illicit sexual urges, they shall continue to rot and decay further in death. They shall battle and wage war against each other and none shall win in this war. In mind of war, they shall have no peace or rest. In their darkness death prison, they will be helpless and hopeless and in their hopelessness, they shall only be in mind to purchase lies and shall hate and extremely despise the Truth. They shall die in eternal prison forever, for they will be unrepentant just like me. No one can escape from my evil rule. Evil shall rule over the world and no one shall believe in Jesus Christ. He shall increasingly become unpopular because I will give humans alternative false doctrines and they shall purchase them with great mind of evil pleasure.

I have commissioned the regiment of wicked lies to spread abundant rumours and lies. I will give them many alternative doctrines that shall destroy humans and humans shall not walk in the light, but in thick darkness. Humans in the world shall do everything that is opposite to the will of God and I will reign supreme. Marriage shall soon be outdated. Sin and iniquity shall increase and wickedness shall rule. The mind of man is fixed on the channels of death and the evil dead shall keep them so much entertained that they shall never think of changing channels from death to life. The world shall not see any light because the order of darkness shall be the order of the world. Evil shall reign and wickedness shall rule, for this is the time of darkness. Know that you cannot win over darkness in the land of darkness. You will only waste your time trying to witness for the Lamb in a world ruled by the wicked.

It is true that the Lamb is the goodness of God revealed, however as you can now clearly see, the world is ruled by evil forces and does not wish to have any goodness. Therefore if your testimony is of the Lamb, you have no chance of surviving whatsoever. Strong opposition is against you, many agents of darkness are everywhere and you are in no way any match for them. Join us and I will set you free, but if you are against us, you will not be free from this realm of darkness, let alone succeed in anything you lay your hands on in this world. I am head of the rulers of the world of darkness and the key to success in the world is in my hand. We know you have a staff and a key in your hand but that key is useless. As you can see, everyone in the world is against you and no one is on your side in this battle. The way to rise or succeed on anything in the world is to join us.

Do not bear testimony of the Lamb as the Lord, for look what happened to the Lamb. The world bruised and nailed Him to His own Cross and made Him carry His Cross upon His own shoulder. Was He able to save Himself from death let alone you? Though it is true that He is the Resurrection, how many people believe in His Gospel of Resurrection today? What good have all His 'good deeds' brought to His name? Does the world not regard Him as a liar? As for your so-called illusive heavenly experience, if heaven so much loves you, why are you back in hell? Why did He not keep you in His heaven to protect you? He abandoned you just when you needed Him most, which is so typical of Him. Now that He has abandoned you, what power do you think you have on your own to fight against me and win? You cannot stop my troops, because they are more than dust and they are everywhere. Save yourself unnecessary suffering and join us, and you will be greatly rewarded with so much money and wealth.

The world is a world of darkness and you cannot testify to the Truth in a world of darkness. The heart of man in the world is only interested in evil and I like to keep it that way. They are not interested in any news of salvation or testimony of life, and even if anyone was remotely interested, what makes you think I will just let you spoil the works my servants of darkness have done with your so-called 'Word' of light? To take you out of your misery, I am going to make you a generous offer and if you are wise you will accept it. I invite you to join me rule the world and I will give you all the riches you cannot even begin to imagine. I know of your financial situation and that your house is about to be repossessed. It will be foolish of you not to take this offer. Think of what you could do with all the world riches at your disposal. You will no longer have to slave yourself, working just to pay off your never decreasing debts. You can pay off all your debts, move into a bigger house, drive around in big cars and have people wait on you instead of slaving yourself around. The secret of the world's wealth is in my hands and if you accept this offer, you can begin to enjoy your life in the real heaven on earth.

There are no guarantees you will eventually make it to the heaven that you saw and besides, look what they did to you; they sent you back to hell with no help whatsoever. You do not have to die in suffering before enjoying yourself. My heaven is real and you can soon begin enjoying yourself if you take my offer. Given the circumstances, you must agree that I am quite generous with this offer I am making you, considering the fact that you are actually my prisoner and you have no means of escape. If you refuse my generous offer, I will destroy you. I will render you penniless, homeless and as a final blow make you insane in the world and when I am done with giving you the real taste of hell on earth—I will take you out to remain in my darkness forever.

Trusting in God right now will not help you. Look what happened to His Only Begotten Son that you consider your Master in the world. If you have a Master that was unable to save Himself from the world of sin back then, how can He save you from a world that is even more sinful today? How do you think I would allow you to spread any truth when we have succeeded in spreading so much lies and most people in the world are now totally blind and deeply buried in the prison of darkness. Stop suffering for nothing. Join me and I will make you a joint ruler in my kingdom of darkness. I will give you control over battalions of demonic regiments and no one will be able to stand against you.

Human beings are nothing but beastly animals. They are only interested in sin. If you join me to promote sin, I will reveal the secrets of the world to you, give you so much power and you will have followers everywhere. However, if you choose to carry on working for God you will get nowhere because no one is interested in God. Besides who will listen to an insane human, because that is exactly what I will turn you into if you refuse my generous offer. Every man must perish in death, for who is man that they should have eternal life when the Lord condemned me to eternal death. Quit deceiving yourself that you will win this battle because you cannot win. Tell us the secret of the power of the Word that is in you and use it for our cause and you shall be greatly rewarded.

If you do not tell us or join us, we will bruise you even more and give you back to the world completely insane. We will take you to the depth of the darkest and hottest place in hell and there the insanity regiment will descend even more upon your physical being and lead you to commit terrible crimes and make you a killer of your fellow-beings. You will spend the rest of your time in the world in a prison for the insane and I will eventually come and get you and make you suffer forever. Tell me, who will believe God has anything to do with an insane murderer? Make up your mind now and save yourself from more trouble. However if you refuse, be rest assured that you have not seen anything called battle yet!

I have gathered false witnesses to testify against you everywhere and you will face terrible trials and be condemned if you do not give up now and join us. You have no idea what and who you are up against. Who do you think you are, trying to battle with the rulers of darkness? I have all power and might to rule the world as I please. I know who you are and I have had my eyes on you to destroy you ever since you came to the world. However everything takes place for a cause and it is better this way, because this way you will be consciously aware that I, Satan have all the power to do as I please. You are nothing and I hold the keys to everything. That little key that you hold in your hands will not open any door for you, but if you accept my offer I will open many doors for you in the world and you will have no limit of wealth, power and fame. Have you not tried and failed to have success in the world? Bow and concede your defeat and I will let you have a kind of success in the world that is beyond your human comprehension.

My stomach churned with so much anger as I listened to his wicked words and upon hearing all he had to say I felt he did not even deserve an answer. My heart could not curtail the extent of his wicked mind and intentions and I felt so sorry for my fellow human beings. Each word was like an arrow in my heart. I was so full of deep, sad emotions to discover that this evil and extremely wicked enemy is unrepentantly determined to destroy every man for no apparent reason. Physically, I felt weaker and weaker as he continued talking and I struggled so much to remain standing due to being very weak. I felt I had to remain in a standing position and not sit down. I kept thinking in my mind that if no ordinary eyes could see this extremely wicked enemy, how would it be possible for any human to escape from his wicked and evil will of intention to destroy? Due to the fact that I had been physically standing for so long, my feet got weaker and I got even thirstier. As I continued to hear of his wicked plans, it further dawned on me that no man had any chance in the world against this wicked enemy except indeed by the grace of God.

My heart felt so sorrowful for the whole of mankind and I started to weep uncontrollably. My response to everything he said was in songs. These songs were no ordinary songs because the moment I started singing them, I had so much strength and greater determination in me to win more than ever before. When I started singing, the battle intensified even more. I felt many missiles in that dark spiritual realm being thrown at me, from all angles at the same time. As the battle intensified, it was as if even though I was winning, I was at the same time sinking deeper into the abyss of darkness. The more the sinking effect, the more bruised and battered I felt; and the more bruised and battered I felt, the weaker I got physically. I also got thirstier and thirstier. The entire world of flesh was in on this battle and both the living dead and the world 'pronounced' dead, wanted me completely buried in hell. People that I thought would support me were against me. It was I against the world and everyone wanted this power of the Lion of Judah, which apparently was in my hand. I heard many voices say, "We will not help you because we want the power too and we cannot let you have it to use against us".

The worst opposition came from both the world's media-regiment and the world's prominent ruling-order regiment. The world media- regiment revealed themselves as the channel waves for the rulers of darkness. They highlighted that their main aim is to pollute people's minds both young and old to conform the minds to sin only. They said their darkness channel-wave agenda is to sell and promote sin and encourage a person to do everything that is against the will of God. At the top of their product lists are bestsellers—witchcraft, vanity and from vanity, debt, violence, magic, pornography, sexual promiscuity of all sorts and false doctrines.

They also tried to convince me that if I joined these rulers of darkness and help promote these products and all other forms of sinful order, the rulers of darkness would greatly reward me. They also said the channel-waves of the world are not for God and that it is for them to use for the proclamation of the agenda of the rulers of darkness that are in high places of the world. They said they are not supporters of godly things because the world is subject to the direct rule of death. They proclaimed that only if I supported the aim of darkness, would they be behind me and even help make me famous across the earth. They said if I joined the darkness order, I would be free from world oppression as they would help package and publicise me to the extent that I would be a 'world idol' and be worshipped by many.

They further said that unless I joined them, no one would notice any of the gifting that I have because I would not have their marketing support or backing. Also, that without their support I would only be wasting my time trying to market any godly talent or gifting, because the world market is only for selling sin and iniquity, not things of 'righteousness'. They said they are the channel wave of fear and not of peace and that they are only interested in proclaiming news of death and not news of resurrection from death. As I continued sinking further into the abyss of darkness, I was able to see more of the faces of the world prominent order regiment and they threw many dart words at me as if that was my punishment for seeing their faces. I heard them in their many numbers say "Now that you know the secret of who we are, you cannot go back to a normal life on earth unless you join us". They said no one sees the secret of evil and escapes from evil rule because evil is a secret that rules from a secret hiding place.

The smell of the physical atmosphere worsened and I was under heavy siege from all corners of the world. It got to a point when I wanted to move forward from my standing position, but my feet were heavy and I could not move them. Although I felt I was winning the battle, it did not seem like I was making any kind of progress and I was beginning to get highly frustrated. Deep in my frustrations, I suddenly remembered the Word of the Great I AM, that all I had to do was, 'Give fear to death' and that once I gave fear to death, I would be free from the realm of darkness that I was in. It seemed as if I had suffered some kind of amnesia in respect to what the Lord had said, but as soon as I remembered what the Lord had said, I heard the wicked voice of Satan say:

Do not deceive yourself. There is no escape from this. You have seen that the world is mine. The world is only interested in wickedness and sin, and no one that has a mind to walk in goodness shall have peace. Evil has taken over the universe and whosoever joins me, I shall give ultimate power and control to rule in the universe forever. Stop wasting your energy. What makes you think you can make a change? God Himself as Word came in flesh and was unable to convince humans to change. If you carry on in the mind to oppose my kingdom of darkness, I will take from you everything you have in the world, strip you naked and destroy you. I will toy with your mind and I will make you confess to things that you have not done. Quit deceiving yourself. Join my many leagues of world champions and start to enjoy heaven on earth. If you join my World Order rule of darkness, I will enable you to be very rich. I will make you a world oppressor not the oppressed that you have been all your life. If you refuse to join me, I will slay you just as I did your Master who as you can see so far has done nothing to help you come out of your rotten position. What profit is there for you to suffer when you can have all the enjoyment of the world?

As he was speaking, I got stronger, unlike before when I felt so weak from hearing all his wicked intentions and plans. In renewed strength and in full remembrance of what I needed to do, I shouted at the top of my voice:

Satan, you are liar and a loser! Christ was bruised for my transgressions. Battered for my iniquities and by His Stripes, I am healed. He carried His Cross and bore my own cross, so I can walk in total victory in everlasting life. He was crucified for my resurrection. He is my righteousness and holiness. He finished the work of my redemption and He is seated at the right hand of the Father as the One who came and conquered the world for me. He has fully redeemed and justified me by His graceful love. By His faithful and loving justification for me, He crossed out every mark of death and gave me His entire 'pass marks' for eternal life. By His grace, I have access to eternal life of light and He has made me light and because He made me light! Darkness cannot keep me down. My soul belongs to the Lord and because I am the Lord's, I am the living and as the living, death cannot keep me locked in the dungeon of death. I am a winner forever.

You are forever a loser and since I am already a winner forever, I am already rich in the Kingdom of God. The wealth of the world is illusion but the Kingdom of God is the kingdom of real wealth and everlasting prosperity. The Lamb already defeated you and I have my victory in the Lamb forever. This battle is not mine; it is the Lord's battle. The Lord already won this battle for me before it even began, and this battle I am having with you is just so that I know that I am victorious in Him—forever. Therefore, I claim and declare my victory, and I give back to you your fear and now I shall rest.

Immediately I said these things, everything subsided. I was physically tired and felt as if I had been on my feet for many years. I was weak, tired and all I wanted to do at this point was physically lie down and have some beautiful, restful sleep. I had not known sleep in what seemed like an eternity and all I wanted was to get on with my life -- now that it seemed everything was peacefully back to normal. As I lay down, ready to drift into some restful sleep, I felt a tap on my shoulder. I opened my eyes and saw a very ugly creature. He said:

> I am one with Satan. I am fear and Satan has refused to have me so I have come back to you. If you have no fear, then you will no longer be afraid in the world and if you are not afraid in the world then how shall he rule over you? It is only by fear that I shall keep you down in the sleep of death. Therefore, I am here to stay and will not go back to Satan.

Upon hearing these words from the ugly creature, I sat up from my bed and immediately started praying aloud. As I went into a loud prayer, many things started happening to me again. Attacks came from everywhere and for several days, I laid in one position with a body heavily laden. I felt paralysed completely and could not move at all from this position. From this heavy-laden position, my eyes were opened to see further revelations. I saw that fear was in my mind because I am flesh and as flesh a sinner. My eyes opened further and I saw a movie picture showing on a huge wide screen before me. I saw myself on the movie screen and a book similar to one of the books of death open. And I saw written in the book my first name and family name, date of birth, place of birth and expected year of death (2003 and cause of death breast cancer).

The book closed and writings started scrolling across the screen. The writings that scrolled across the screen seemed to be telling a story, to make me see who I was and how I had gotten to where I was at that moment. It began by saying that I was a descendant of the first Adam and as a descendant of the first

Adam; I had entered into an unholy covenant with Satan through the sin of the first Adam. In this covenant of sin, I was spiritually dead and imprisoned in my soul. I had so many fears and listed were all the kinds of fears that I had, and I saw that the ultimate fear that I had was of death. The main reason for my fears was that I was conceived in sin, and in sin, in darkness realm of fear. As the writings kept scrolling across, I saw a picture of myself in a small place that looked like a prison cell and in this place, I looked so afraid. I heard myself repeatedly saying "Unless my soul wakes-up I am going to be in this place forever".

The story continued scrolling across to reveal more information; that even though I wanted to be free, but because I was dead and sinful—my heart was focused on vanity. In my heart of vanity and flesh desires, I was against the only Truth that would afford me my salvation. In sinful death, I was only in mind of fleshy desires and such desires only worked to further corrupt my soul. With a corrupt soul, I was in denial of the loving sacrifice that God made to free me from the covenant of sin. I was unable to understand the purpose of Christ's birth, death and resurrection. In sin every human as a descendant of the first Adam became subject to the rule of darkness.

Although God sentenced man just as He did the principality-angels to serve time with hard labour, He showed mercy unto man from His eternal existence. God gave man His grace in the 'era' of time, to rehabilitate them for eternal life's sake. However, man in time-era was unable to see the grace and love of God because in the fall into sin, man became anti-God and pro-evil.

The darkness realm rulers of principalities are fallen angels from heaven. These fallen angels as aliens from heaven became spirits of temptation and as spirits of temptations, wicked enemies of humans. Their main aim is to rule humans in the dark prison of death, so that humans will never again see the glory of God. Their main strategy is confusion. They cunningly package confusion and sell it to mankind in the world for the sake of turning human beings against each other and against God. The dark ruling-principalities are aliens and time-realm wanderers. These principalities are rulers of darkness who have all journeyed to the time- era, in order to erect temples of confusion to keep the soul of man in monumental darkness prison of death everlastingly. They all came in rotation order in the era of time in different kinds of shapes and forms, in order to give different kinds of false doctrines and ideas to humans all the way to the end of time. They sent their agents to spread many fables to deeply confuse humans, and to make it impossible for them to see the only way to the true God.

The scrolling information continued on the screen to reveal that just as all the principality-heads of darkness journeyed to confuse man, God also as the Head of all principalities and powers journeyed into time from His eternal existence in the form of Christ—to give man certainty of life and eternal freedom from death. Christ is the righteous, flesh and blood of God who knew no sin and He is the loving heart of God. Even though He knew no sin, He chose to die as sin because sin is the password for entering into the realm of darkness. However, as the righteousness of God, He arose from death and became the door of salvation for mankind. He is the only door that can lead mankind from darkness to light. He is light and as light, He shines forever. He came to give mankind the heart of God and set man free from the heart of darkness and evil. Human beings in the world in the wicked heart of sin tried and found Christ guilty of blasphemy, which is a sin punishable by death. This was all in the will of God to show human beings God's divine ways

of Justice. Human beings in the world in the wicked heart of sin tried and found Christ guilty of blasphemy which is a sin punishable by death. This was all in the Will of God to show Human beings God's

He who knew no sin could not be in condemnation of death because only a soul who sins shall perish in death. Those who accused Christ of blasphemy were guilty already of sin and unless redeemed by Christ the sinless tried, they will be eternally subject to the penalty for blasphemy—which is eternal condemnation in death. Christ is the holiness of God revealed and it is only by His blood that any human being shall be free from the condemnation of sin. Christ is the way to eternal life of peace and just as He journeyed to earth to afford humans the redemption from sin through His death and resurrection, He shall return at the end of time to give His final judgement to all. Those whom He finds in sin upon His return, He shall pronounce permanently dead. For the one who was tried as sin, is RIGHTEOUSNESS and as RIGHTEOUSNESS, He is the only advocate of life, the first and last judge.

As the words, 'the first and last judge' finished scrolling across the screen, the written words stopped. Instead of scrolling words, a picture of Christ's image appeared as men were nailing Him to the Cross. Around Him was an angry mob. I saw myself as one of those in the mob and we were shouting, 'Crucify Him'. As I was shouting, 'Crucify Him' I saw a message written in bold letters flash on the screen saying:

To crucify Him is the will and intention of God, but to crucify and deny Him as the RIGHTEOUSNESS of God is

a crime against the universal ruling order of life. Penalty for rejecting the Righteousness of life is eternal death.

Immediately after the bold writings, I saw Christ calling me from a distance saying that I should repent, and that if I repent He would forgive me all my sins. However, each time I wanted to look His way, a huge brick wall will drop down from nowhere in front of me and written on the wall were the words:

REJECT HIM AND ENJOY YOUR LIFE!

Then some scrolling words came back on immediately to reveal that I was in denial of the only Truth that could set me free, because I saw sin as pleasurable and righteousness as boring. It carried on revealing that in blindness of death, I had no real knowledge of good and evil and I lacked true knowledge of life. I was carnal in my thinking and self-justifying within myself, which only worked to condemn my soul further, for God is the only justifier. I was self-righteous and against God's own righteousness. I could not see the need for repentance, for I believed I was a just and righteous person.

The scroll at this point again stopped, and I saw myself on the screen in a cage-like room looking very filthy and dirty. The wall of this cage-room was all dark coloured and I saw writing on the walls that said: "Enemy of the truth in denial of her sins, predestined to awake and have extra time for the glory of God". Then followed by bold letters I saw written these words:

KEEP ON A SPECIAL WATCH!

The picture of me in the cage became minimised and there was a larger picture of me walking around the earth's surface. I had many objects looking like placards in my hands and straightaway started displaying the placards one after the other in slow motion as if I was making some sort of presentation to an audience. Written on the placards was everything I had ever said against Jesus. The placards were like never ending records of many of the things I had said or done since I had been on earth. Finally I had what appeared to be the last placard in my hand. On it was written:

If there is a heaven and hell and I end up in hell I will deal with it when I get there.

The screen froze with me holding this placard. Now in my conscious reality of what hell is really like, I could not help but shed many tears from watching my frozen image on the screen now holding a placard that contained words I wished I had never said. I remembered making the statement on the last placard in response to someone who once said that I should give my life to Christ so that I do not perish in hell. With my eyes fixed on the frozen image of me holding this placard on the screen I became very sad, because I could now see that hell was not something I could deal with by any means.

I felt so terrible and deeply emotional with the revelations of these things and I wept bitterly. Somehow, I felt like the greatest criminal of all time that does not deserve Christ's forgiveness. I felt like a traitor and betrayer. I opened my mouth and with tears flowing like an ocean onto my face, I started to repeatedly confess Christ as my Saviour. I begged that He shows us all His mercy; for all that we had done to wrongly repay Him for His loving kindness toward us all. As soon as I had finished my confession and deep apology to Christ and also repented on behalf of the entire human race, I heard a soft friendly voice say:

Your victory is already yours. All you had to do was claim it. The key to your freedom is your heart of confession and in your goodness heart of confession; you are forever free from death. You are in freedom and in goodness of life. The record that you had in the book of death is of no effect against your soul. For though death had destined you to physically die in 2003 never to wake-up again from spiritual death, I had predestined you to wake-up from death that same year and remain in awakening forevermore for my glory sake. By grace, I have made you to be light, and darkness cannot prevail over light for light is a ruler over darkness. Your trials are all working out for the goodness of your soul. I have predestined you to overcome in your trials and tribulations in order to be a perfect witness and vessel of goodness in the end-time, for my judgement day is at hand. I have allowed your trials to afford your soul full knowledge of justification. I have given you full victory in your trials to assure you of my eternal love.

I created you to be My witness out of My graceful heart and I as a witness to your confession; I decree you justified in all dominion and dimensional realms. Rejoice for in this day you will know that I am truly Your Lord and Saviour. You have declared your loyalty to goodness and have rejected evil. This is the test of righteousness, to know good and evil and choose: good. By grace, I afford you My 'pass marks', and abolish every mark of the beast upon your soul. I have deemed you an agent of life to have eternal rewards of life forever. As an agent of life, I deem you light and as light, your record and name shall always be in the Book of Life. Now as light, get ready to speak in total light and proclaim the Good News of love in all corners of the world, for I am with you in all dominion and dimensional realms— now and forevermore. Therefore, Daughter of Zion, fear no more for I am with you always. Arise and walk in your total victory.

Immediately after He finished speaking these Words, I spoke for the first time with a voice full of confidence like never before. This voice sounded nothing like my normal voice. It was a voice full of power and authority.

I then spoke in a loud voice and said, "Satan! I am free from every unholy covenant now and forever".

He responded by saying, "By what authority do you do this? A covenant is a covenant and in sinful covenant. You belong to death"!

Full of some amazing confidence, I shouted:

Silence! Although I was conceived in sin, I am now in Christ without sin, for I am now born again of the Spirit of God. This battle is the Lord's and He has given me victory. I have nothing further to say to you for Jesus is Lord and in His power, every knee must bow and every tongue in heaven and on earth must confess that Jesus Christ is Lord in all dimensional dominion realms. So I now command you in the Name of Jesus get thee behind me.

After this, I turned my attention to God and started crying unto Him saying:

O Lord in Your power You raised me up from the dead to dwell in Your presence everlastingly. I know that You have freed me from hell, but so that I may go into the world and do your will as You predestined me. Open O Lord the gates of hell for me that I may come out. You promised not to leave any part of me in hell. Christ You are my Lord and Saviour and I believe if you say the Word, the gate will open. For all power and authority is in Your Word. I now see that your Word is the Key and Staff of authority in my hand. I believe O Lord Jesus in your power, and I believe You died and resurrected as my Saviour and that You are in me as the Holy Spirit of life.

Open the gate O Lord and save me from the thirst of hell. For long, I have been on trial from the darkness realm of the world but by Your grace, You have already pre-justified me to overcome the world. Release me now Lord from the confinement of sorrowful darkness, and let every part of me rejoice in Your Holy presence. O Lord, my Holy Redeemer, release me for I thirst and am weak. My legs wobble and they are physically weak. The enemy tried to compress me with the heavy laden of fear. My body is shaky and my eyes are red. My mind was sorrowful in my trials and I saw O my Redeemer that I cannot bear the punishment of sin. The smell of hell chokes me, for the body of death is terrible and decomposed in wickedness. False witnesses gather around me to force me to confess in the world of humans that I am an evildoer. Arise! O Lord now, in Your consuming fire, and open the door of Your glory fully in my life. Open the door of Your heavenly glory for me and free me completely from darkness. For all the power, O great Redeemer is Yours, the honour and the glory now and forevermore.

After I had finished saying these words, I heard a voice say loudly:

Satan! The battle is over. Her loyalty is unto goodness and despite facing extreme trials; she has showed solidarity unto goodness. She has held on to her belief in Me—that I am her personal Lord and Saviour. She was never for a moment willing to let go of her belief in Me, even when it seemed as if I was no longer there for her. Her trials are over, for she has authority. In Me is all authority and this authority's Name is I JESUS. She has given her life to Me and I have pre-justified her to live. She has declared herself on the side of 'goodness' and rejected 'evil'. Therefore she is a witness in goodness free to testify for goodness sake in the world to the end of the world. She is the winner and Satan you are once again now and forevermore the loser. Now let honours of victory follow her as the winner, and let shame follow you the loser.

Then I heard Satan say with a weepy voice:

The Lord rebukes me to perish in eternal damnation. Yet He gave grace unto mankind who like me are also sinners. No human can stand against darkness without You O Lord and because You have given her grace of victory, she is a winner forevermore. Your will must be done for who am I, O Lord to question Your will and decisions. For as the Great I AM that You Are, unto You be all the glory, the honour and all the power. Victory belongs unto whom the Lord gives victory and defeat belongs unto whom the Lord gives defeat.

At this point, I saw the big screen appear again. This time the entire picture of the world with Satan in it appeared and with head bowed, he said: "O Lord Christ, You are the King of kings and as the Kings of kings Yours is the kingdom, the Power and Glory now and forevermore". And his face disappeared from the screen. As soon as his picture disappeared, I saw the picture of Christ fill the whole screen and He said:

Satan, your secret is out forever. You are forever in disgrace for you are a betrayer of loving goodness. Shame unto you forever you evil counterfeiter. For trying the saints, I will increase the flame of hell, and pain and sorrow will increase in your soul forever. Hear O ye people of the world, I Christ, I am love and as love, the Lord of victory everlasting. Love is the Word of perfect creation. Love is light and love as light is the ordinance power of life. Love is peace, rest and joy. Love is the Truth and only the Truth shall set humans free. Before the foundation of the world, Satan was a betrayer and as a betrayer of love, he will never again have the goodness of love. Those that follow darkness will perish everlastingly in the burning lake of fire that burns without end. I am the Way, the Truth and Life and all that follows Me shall walk in My victory over death forever. As it was in the beginning, so it is and shall ever be eternal life only in love without end forever and ever. Now let there be light.

When He finished saying these words, I saw appearing on the screen gradual images of creation. I saw the sea gathered and land appear. I saw all kinds of animals appear then I saw a man appear and after the man, a woman appeared on the screen. The environment was beautiful and they both looked joyfully perfect. Then came into the scene Satan and soon after, the perfect picture turned ugly. After a series of what seemed like everlasting violent ugly pictures, the picture of Christ on the Cross, appeared, and when He had said, 'It is finished' the entire screen went blank and there were no further pictures. Then I heard Him say:

Daughter of Zion, all prophecy is fulfilled ahead of time but so that all see the reality of the big picture; everything as it is will be revealed at the appointed time. All is well that ends well. Now in total victory of life, open your mouth and prophesy the goodness testimony of My name. For the testimony of I, Christ is indeed the Spirit of life prophecy.

I opened my mouth and began to say:

I have the authority of the Father, the Son and the Holy Ghost. Jesus Christ is Lord of victory everlasting and His victory belongs to me forever. Now open O ye doors, for the Lord of Glory is in me and no gates of hell can stand in the way of the Lord of Glory.

As soon as I finished saying these words, I saw the gate of hell open. As I walked through the gates, simultaneously, the heavy-laden that was upon me in the visible lifted, and I could once again rise on my feet and walk. In the invisible dimension, at the other side of the gate—was the Lord Jesus Christ shining and looking as beautiful as ever. He looked toward me and smiled. Then He said:

So that all things as written concerning you are recorded in all realms as fulfilled, your trials in the world will continue. This is necessary for greater revelation and perfect conviction of your revelations. Persevere for it will only be for a short while. I have overcome the world; therefore no matter what the case might be always remember that it is all working together for the goodness of your soul. Now as it is written, go into all realms and declare your victory and it is well with your soul now and forevermore.

CHAPTER FIVE
REVELATIONS OF SECOND COMING

"And I saw the dead, small and great, stand before God; and the books were opened: and another book was opened, which is the book of life: and the dead were judged out of those things which were written in the books, according to their works. And the sea gave up the dead which were in it; and death and hell delivered up the dead which were in them: and they were judged every man according to their works. And death and hell were cast into the lake of fire. This is the second death. And whosoever was not found written in the book of life was cast into the lake of fire".

—Revelation 20:12-15

As soon as I was visibly able to rise on my feet, I began pacing up and down the house again and this was due to the fact that my spirit was still in full vision of my invisible realm revelations and nothing appeared normal still in the natural world. The Lord opened my eyes to continue to see more of His revelations. In my follow up revelation, the Lord opened my eyes to see events of the last days of time, and of the Day of Judgement. He showed me the hour of the clock and I could see that the hands of time had long stopped at midnight and will remain at midnight until the Son of God arrives. As the hand was about to move past midnight which is the sign that the King of kings is about to appear in all His Glory, I saw some dark angels gather in battle gear to battle so that all that is written, is seen in all realms as fulfilled. I heard the angels of darkness say, "The Lamb shall now come as the Almighty to judge us and it is all over for us when He comes".

The moment the dark angels had finished gathering themselves together and ready to battle, I saw the presence of an angel of God on earth filled with great power from God. He started singing and his songs were like a trumpet sound to announce the coming of the Son of Man, who is the Son of God. As I began to hear the angel sing, I broke out in victory song in 'tongues of fire' (Acts 2:1-4). I felt a sudden urge to go outside the house to sing in the open space of the earth. I went outside the house in total confidence in the Lord and started to sing the victory song in tongues of fire. As I began singing, my voice came forth so loud in the open space and sounded as if it was travelling around the whole earth and this is the interpretation of the song:

Lord, You are Holy. Lord, You are Holy. In this day, You have given me victory and I will declare Your goodness across the earth. In this day You have judged me in Your righteousness and established me in Your holiness. Eternal graceful Father, You are merciful and I praise You now and forever. Hosanna and hallelujah shall be my song in Zion, the city of lights that never go dark. Your Glory O Lord is the light of Your city. The Lord is good, I know, and His goodness endures now and forevermore.

The Lord gave me the victory of the Lamb to have His resurrection power of eternal life. This is Your grace and goodness unto me and it is for Your glory's sake O Lord of

Hosts. I will rejoice in Zion for the Lord is my pillar and my shield. Never again shall my soul suffer death, for the Lord of Zion is the pillar of my life. The Lord King of Glory is with me in all His glory and for the goodness of His Holy Name, He has redeemed my soul from death.

I have victory in the Name of Christ Jesus. Christ You are Lord and when I mention Your name, Your goodness glory shines bright upon me. At the mentioning of Your name, my enemies bow in their everlasting defeat. At the mentioning of Your Name all knees are bowed and every tongue in heaven and on the earth declares that Jesus, You are Lord. You have made me a champion everlastingly and out of Your grace of love, You have abolished death for me. Your light and glory shine upon me everlastingly and in Your light, darkness has no power over my soul.

HOLY, HOLY and HOLY is the Name of the Lamb that washed my sins away now and forever. With Your holy blood, you washed me and made me to be as white as snow.

Hosanna to the King of kings, the God Who was, Who is and Who reigns supreme everlastingly. The Lord comes in His chariot of fire, with all His angels to give shame to the beast and eternal reward of life to the saints. How wonderful are You O King of Glory? You are love and as my love and master in all dominion, You came from Your heavenly glory to save me from the world of sinful death. You are the defender of faith and I bear witness and give testimony that You are the Holy Redeemer of life that can place us all in goodness glory of eternal life. O King of kings, Alpha and

Omega, great is Your faithfulness, yesterday, today and forever.

All the angels and saints sing hallelujah to the Lord of lords. You are worthy Lord of all praises and worship, and in this day I worship You in my soul and spirit. You are Alpha and Omega, and Glory be to Your Name forever and ever. Glory be to the Father, the Son and the Holy Ghost. As it was in the beginning, so it is now that the Lord only is our victory as life, love, peace, joy and rest in eternity. Glory be to You O Great I AM. Unto You is all honour, all glory and power now and forevermore.

Blessed be the Name of the Lord, forever.
Blessed be the Name of the Lamb our Holy Redeemer who died, resurrected, and lives forever as light of the universe.
Holy is the Name of the Father, the Son and the Holy Ghost. Amen.

As I continued singing my songs of victory in 'tongues of fire' in the open space, my neighbours, spiritually motivated, but acting physically had called the police. However, by the time the police arrived I had gone back inside the house. I knew the police were coming, because I heard a spirit say, "We have called the police for you and soon you will be taken to the hospital for the insane for disturbing us". When the police arrived at my doorstep and I opened the door for them, I saw that they had heads of wolves but I was not afraid anymore. The spirit hibernating in the visible body of one of the police officers said, "You will soon be taken to the hospital for the insane for disturbing us".

However, the human audible voice coming from the officers said something different. They said someone had called them to say I was disturbing the peace of the neighbourhood. In understanding of everything that was going on as the Lord had enabled me, I gave my vocal answer to the natural statement and not to the silent spiritual words. I knew that to respond to the silent spiritual threats would sound inappropriate, and mad in the ordinary sense of mind, and as such, I responded in the normal tone to the normal question and said, I was not disturbing the peace. I had the spirit again say:

Your trials have only just begun. You may have won in the spirit world but we would soon see how well you can handle the trials of the visible world of flesh. You will soon be on your way to the hospital for the insane—but not yet. We will go now, but we will soon be back.

In the visibly audible dimension, the police officers, who were now acting as the channel vessel for the evil spirit world of darkness said they would leave, but may have to return if they get any more reports from the neighbours; that I am, 'Disturbing the peace'. After they left, I continued to see more revelations. I heard the angel with the voice of the Trumpet still singing and saw that the fallen angels had gathered to stop him. As the angel continued to sing and the fallen angels were trying to stop him, I saw one with a white banner whom I recognised as Michael and with him all the other archangels. They came from heaven, full of the fire of the Holy Ghost to battle and destroy all the wicked dark angels and to prepare the way for the coming of the Lord. In this particular hour of battle, complete darkness fell upon the earth.

No light came from heaven down to earth. The moon or the sun did not rise to shine upon the earth. This moment of complete darkness on the earth signalled the closing of the Ark and completion of era of Grace. Satan and all the dark angels were visible in the clouds and fear gripped all humans on the earth. I saw all fallen stars of heaven falling from the clouds to the ground. Michael and the other archangels tortured them with their flaming sword for attempting to stand in the way of the coming of the Lord. The whole of the earth was in total chaos and there was much wailing and weeping. I saw human beings running around everywhere, crying for the Lord to save them, but it was now too late because darkness was upon the world and the Day of the Lord had come. At the end of the darkness hour, which was three days, the voice of the angel became louder. The victorious angels of the Lord had captured all the wicked fallen angels and had placed them in a thing that looked like a cage but also looked like a net for the final throwing of their bodies into the abyss lake of fire HELL.

On the last day and at the final hour of time, heaven opened and the light of the glory of the Son of God filled the earth. I saw the sky filled with the angels of heaven and they were uncountable in number. They sang to the sound of many harps and other musical instruments. The voices of the angels filled the earthly globe and I heard the voices of the angels singing powerful and great songs of joy across the heavens and the earth. At this moment, the angel with the voice like a Trumpet finished his song and the total number of songs was a thousand and one.

When he ended the song, it was exactly one second past the midnight hour of time in eternal calculations. Then, the Son of Man being the Son of God and the Son of God, GOD; appeared in a chariot of fire. He sat as THE JUDGE on His Throne of Judgement. Bright lights filled the skies and the fire of God's Glory lit the whole earth. I heard the voice of the Lord call out every spirit in the universe unto order for judgement. Every spirit appeared lining for judgement. They came from everywhere—from under the ground, the sea, the ocean and all alien spirits of the universe that God had banished from heaven before the foundation of the world. All dead spirits in hell came and the human spirit beings who were physically on earth at that time all gathered for judgement. Many were in tears for they said: "Now we know that Jesus really is Lord".

As the King of kings started to speak, all spirits bowed their heads before Him and proclaimed glory be to the Father and to the Son and to the Holy Ghost. Then with a loud voice, the Son of Man being the Son of God commanded: "Satan! Reveal yourself for Man to see". At the commanding tone of the Lord's voice, the gates of hell opened and Satan appeared in a cage made of steels of fire. He looked ugly beyond description. He bowed and said:

Surely goodness is the only thing that pays. As the first and last to sin, I am the first and last to receive condemnation from the Lord. I have deceived humans due to their vanity desires. I have troubled man for they are wicked-hearted, greedy in their nature and very foolish in their minds. I have destroyed many for they think of themselves as gods in their own right. The Son of God is God, and the God of the heavens and the Earth is love. The Lord denied me His loving peace as punishment for betraying His love. I cannot have peace and rest for I am evil hearted. I deserve condemnation for I am condemned in my own evil and all that is wicked just like me shall join me today.

The Son of God is God. Almighty Power is Your Name forever. I pay homage to love, for with Your love You redeemed the soul of man from sinful death. No one is able to redeem but You, and since You have not redeemed my soul, it shall forever be in darkness. This is Your judgement O Great One of the universe and no one can reverse Your order of judgement, for you are the first and last judge. As the defeated, I bow before You O Lord of everlasting victory. Jesus Christ is Lord in all dominion and dimensional realms. You are the Alpha Lord and Omega Lord, the Word. You are the Power and as the Holy Spirit the all powerful in everlasting life.

As he finished, he started to wail and weep and for some reason he became uglier and uglier—the more he wept. The Son of God as God then declared:

Now you can see the face of the wicked and the shame of the evil-hearted. The gates of hell I will shut forever and no one again shall be able to come out. The wicked that are just like Satan shall suffer forever in the eternal lake of hell fire and there shall be no more redemption of souls in hell. Now let My witnesses be on My right side and let those who are for the devil go to the left side to perish with the devil forever.

Many immediately tried to rush to the right side of the Son of God who is God, and as God the judge. However, the fierce looking angels that were on guard stopped them with swords of fire. Many started to say, "Master we love You and we bore witness of You only. Please take us and let us be in Your glorious kingdom of love to serve You forever". Then I heard Satan say:

I know you all by name and today you shall join me in my suffering for eternity as reward for your evil. You have wined and dined with evil, now be brave to receive the reward for your evil. I have the books of death and your names and records are in it. Only if your record is in the Book of Life is your record of death nullified. I know your faces and I know that your record of death is still a valid record, for you have sold your souls to me because your hearts were wicked and evil. No more redemption on the day of judgement but rewards says the Lord. Let Your will be done O Lord and let me have the souls of the wicked as my own reward for my own wickedness. Today your reward from the Lord all ye friends of evil is ETERNAL condemnation in the lake of eternal fire.

I also heard many saying, "Satan, you are a liar and we do not know you, for it is the Lord Jesus whose Name we proclaim in our days on earth". Satan responded:

I am a liar alright, but you have found out just when it is too late to be able to have freedom from lies by the power of the true and Holy Redeemer of life. Let Your will be done O Lord and let me have my reward which is the souls of the wicked to partake in my suffering in the eternal lake of fire.

Then the Son of God who is God and as God the judge said:

I know of every record. I am the keeper of the Book of Life and I know what is in the book of death, for as Almighty God of the universe I have all power and authority over all matters of life and death. Whosoever's name is not in the

Book of Life is not of Me and whosoever is not of Me is of death. Today in My final judgement, Satan shall have as reward for his wickedness the souls of the wicked to perish with him in the lake of fire everlastingly and there shall never again be redemption for those souls. Now let the names in the Book of Life be read.

As soon as He finished saying these Words, a large book appeared from His heart, with records of spiritual names written in blood. As He called out the names, those that heard their names jumped with joy, and spoke with one voice saying:

Holy is the Name of the Lamb Who is the Almighty, who by grace has justified us. Though we faced many trials and were truly tested, we had confidence that we are victorious in the Lamb of God. The Lord rewards us today with His eternal profits of goodness for we persevered in long-suffering. The Lamb carried us through the storms of the world. In His faith and by His faithful love, He washed us clean and we are as white as snow. Jesus You are our Lord—now and forever. In Your love, You have made us worthy again to eat from the tree of life. In Your love, You gave us knowledge of life and made way for us to dwell in the eternal presence of the Father. In Your love, You made us sons of the Father to dwell in Your Holy Spirit presence now and forever. Praise and glory be unto You, O Lord everlastingly.

From the countless spirits lined-up before the Lord those whose names were in the Book of Life were relatively few in number. The majority of the spirits who lined up before the Lord did not have their names in the Book of Life. When Satan opened the first 'book of death', it contained the names of all the principality-heads whose names were not in the Book of Life before the foundation of the world. Each principality-head had in their hand a book of death. As Satan finished calling all the names of the heads of principalities, they too opened their books to call out the names written in them. Those whose names were in the books of death shed gut-wrenching tears and begged and pleaded, but it was too late said the Son—who is Word and as Word the Great I AM, the judge of the universe and the defender of the faithful.

Only the obedient child shall inherit the Kingdom of Heaven, says the Lord. Have I not said unto you many times, let those who have ears, hear? Did you not continue in your wicked ways and is it not a divine principle of justice that you reap what you sow? All days are mine for I am the Ancient of Days and today is a day I set aside to reward all spirits according to their ways. As prisoners of time, you greatly tried the righteous, instead of repenting and become free everlastingly from the eternal condemnation of death. Eternal reward of life belongs to the saints for their perseverance and patience in good faith during their time-era existence. Justice is for the good on deeds and the good on deeds are everlasting sons of I the: I AM that I AM—the greatest on all deeds. I command all books to close for all things as written in the beginning are now fulfilled forever and ever. Let the door to the abyss of fire open and let the wicked have the rewards of their wickedness, which is to perish forever.

As soon as the Lord finished saying His Words, in a simultaneous sequence, a huge net made of fire appeared and captured Satan in his cage and also all the others on the left. Then a fire door opened and a sea of fire appeared. The net that captured everyone on the left went straight into the sea of fire and the door and the sea disappeared. Then the Lord said, "Now let the new earth and the new heaven come to light and let the celebrations begin". Just as the Lord commanded, the door to the heaven of the seventh-glory opened and the amazingly beautiful new earth appeared—filled with the light of God's glory.

The Lord opened the gates of the new heaven and earth for all those whose names were in the Book of Life to enter with Him and rest and abide with Him forever. The angels of heaven—which were uncountable in number rejoiced with the saints. They marched on the streets of the New Jerusalem, the city of lights. The city was paved with beautiful precious stones and the Lord revealed the entire beauty of the new heaven and the new earth for the eyes of all the saints to see. There was much joyful singing as the glory of God filled the new heaven and the new earth as light, lighting up the whole place. From seeing this revelation, I became certain of my victory and in certainty cried out "I am free. I have eternal life victory in the Name of Jesus and no matter what the world throws at me; the Lord has assured me that my victory is permanent". In revelation knowledge of my victory, I became even more determined to walk in that victory permanently.

CHAPTER SIX

REVELATIONS OF
THE WORLD ORDER OF SIN

"And deceiveth them that dwell on the earth by the means of those miracles which he had power to do in the sight of the beast; saying to them that dwell on the earth, that they should make an image to the beast, which had the wound by a sword, and did live. And he had power to give life unto the image of the beast, that the image of the beast should both speak, and cause that as many as would not worship the image of the beast should be killed. And he causeth all, both small and great, rich and poor, free and bond, to receive a mark in their right hand, or in their foreheads:

And that no man might buy or sell, save he that had the mark, or the name of the beast, or the number of his name. Here is wisdom. Let him that hath understanding count the number of the beast: for it is the number of a man; and his number is Six hundred threescore and six".

—Revelation 13:14-18

I continued to receive more revelations and even though at that time the revelation experience had been ongoing for what must have been days, it seemed like it had been for a longer period. I no longer had any recollection of time or year and even though I could see my 'normal' surroundings, none of it looked like the world, as I had known it before. My husband, who was a witness to my visible actions and reactions, had no understanding of what was going on. After I had been indoors for what seemed like weeks, I heard him suggest that we go for a drive to get some fresh air. As we drove around, the Lord continued to open my eyes to see more of His revelations and I immediately knew that my husband taking me for a drive was all part of God's plan. The World Order picture that the Lord was now showing me as we drove around was beyond my wildest thoughts or ideas.

The first thing I noticed in this segment of God's revelation was that the clouds were no longer just clouds, but a picture of several images. The main image looked like a beastly creature and it had three separate bodies joined to one head. The three bodies had seven tails. Let the wise count the number of the heads and tails and it is ten. This ten symbolises a unity of the sinful order to indicate that the World Order man and the beast will come together with the intention of taking the entire world into a ground zero of hell.

The image that had three heads and seven tails also had two hands. He was carrying something that looked like a huge baseball bat in both hands. The two hands are symbolic of the minute and hour of time and although they go round and round, time does not actually move. Being that time in the real sense is actually stationary and non-moving, all souls locked into 'time-era' only end up going round and round in labour circles of death acquiring zero returns from their fieldwork in the world. Unless the Lord redeems the sinner, the sinner's final answer will be zero. The mark of zero is the mark of death and those that have a zero mark cannot trade to profit, for there can be no profit in evil. As I looked more closely at the clouds, I saw images of the world's prominent faces all around the beast. They were busy performing all manners of rituals and making all kinds of ritualistic signals that are intended to bring the beast back to life, so that they can reign together with him forever. I saw that they intend to bring the beast back to life through a combination of some strange blood-rituals and channelling-chanting. I saw them perform many blood-rituals for the sake of bringing the beast back to life and I heard much chanting from the World Order images surrounding the image of the beast.

God opened my eyes to see the entire earth globe and I saw many more strange looking creatures walking around the earth. I saw many creatures with heads like wolves and they were all involved in some form of chanting that is meant to bring the beastly image back to life. The terrible smell of the atmosphere became stronger and every one of the strange looking creatures was on a mission to create chaos and disorderliness. The chanting was loud and came from everywhere. It sounded like loud humming. As we drove around it grew louder and louder and I soon realised that the humming chant was a form of strange number counting. God revealed to me that this counting was for the purpose of bringing complete darkness to the earth. They began counting at number six and ended at six. Once they reached the end they would start counting again from six. They counted repeatedly with their eyes fixed on the sky with the hope of bringing darkness to earth at the end of each counting round. I saw that those engaged in the chanting held in their hands some sea-symbols, which represented every number of the beast. They kept on looking up to the sky and also bowing their heads to the ground—frantically looking for signs of the beast, awakening.

Everyone on the street looked strange and was acting strange—all busy gathering the symbols for the chants and kept looking to the sky for signs of darkness reign. The ugly looking creatures were everywhere throughout the world and thirsty for blood. They mostly wanted the blood so they could give it to the beast to drink. They had as their world chanting headquarters a dark, secretive place. In this place many gathered and lined-up to be marked with the special mark of the beastly creature. As soon as they received their mark, a special chain would appear and chain their hands and legs. Once the shackles are attached onto their hands and legs, they became like robotic machines walking round and round in circles of death, pushed around by the hands of death that goes back and forth as the labour-hands of time.

With the shackles tightly in place on their hands and legs, they appeared hypnotised to engage only in endless counting and chanting. Their eyes were constantly fixed to the sky for signs of the 'awakening' of the beast. The chanting is actually a curse to their souls, but they see it as blessings. The more they see it as blessings the more they chant—repeatedly, enabling more of the darkness from the image headquarters to overshadow their minds. In deep-darkness they walk around in blind-fury looking for whom to offer to the beast, for him to devour. The creatures that were all over the world had different shapes, colours and sizes. Some had two heads with eyes in the middle of their foreheads. Thick darkness covered the many heads marked with the special zero mark of the beast. However, because they are all blind, they saw their world of darkness as a world of light.

I saw a church at the centre of the world called the 'Church of Mystery Babylon'. It had many ugly looking heads marked with the special 'mark' of the beast. They sat in the highest places of the world unnoticed, unseen by anyone for whom they really are in the spirit. Their main role is to stand as a barrier in the way of humans to prevent them from seeing the real church of God. They sat in their mystery Babylonian congregation and many wore garments decorated with all kinds of images that appeared holy. They stood at the centre of the world saying, "We are wives of the beast and we have come to deceive the world for the beast's sake". Although this is what they were saying, no one could ordinarily hear their real words. From the ordinary mind perspective, they sounded like they were preaching the Word of God, but in deep revelation, God opened my eyes to see that their real words were coming from their hands, not their mouth.

They communicated in codes and signs. No one from an ordinary eye and mind perspective is able to see or understand the codes and signs. They claim to be followers of Christ, but everything they do is to blaspheme the Name of Christ. They wore on their heads world crowns, made with many fake stones. These words were inscribed on their crowns:

Woe to Mystery Babylon and Unto the World of Sin

God opened my eyes to see a world full of several bloodthirsty darkness-cults, engaged in various kinds of abominable sacrifices and evil sexual practices. The highest cults in the world are for the world's prominent rulers of darkness. These prominent rulers of darkness are the main poisonous tails of the beast. They work tirelessly to bring the entire principality-heads of the beast to the surface of the visible physical world, in order to build a similar, invisible-hell government tracing system, so that no man will serve God, let alone see the ruling loving-system of God.

God further opened my eyes to see the workings of the hell-system that the world-order of humans seeks -- to replicate on the surface of the world. Under the sea-hell-system, every spirit of hell has a special tracking-device attached to their soul. Wherever they are in the world, they are visible to the ruling order of hell. Since they are visible, they cannot hide from the rulers of darkness who are hiding in the high places of the world. Each spirit of hell is a time traveller and as time travellers, they are on evil missions to Earth. Their main mission is to help bring the chaotic, disorderly darkness and ungodly system of hell to the surface of the world. Each hell-regiment visitor has a destined, limited period of stay in the world to perform his or her evil mission.

To ensure that every spirit returns to their hell-family-regiment at their allocated time from their exit point on earth, each hell-family- regiment tags every visitor to the world with a special spiritual 'tracking-device'. They attach this tracking-device to the soul of the visitor coming to the world and the device connects the soul of the time traveller to the soul of the heads of the regiments who are in the dungeon. Through this 'soul-to-soul' connecting device, the invisible hell-regimental-heads are able to control the visible-being throughout their entire journey on earth.

The hell-family-regiment maintains their contacts and control by mind and choice manipulations; mostly through evil dreams and imaginary pictures. With the soul connection device firmly in place, the visitor from hell who is born into the world as a human, but unconscious of his hell-family root connections, will usually follow his hell-family-regiment blueprints designed for him to follow in his entire life-journey on earth.

If the spirit of the visitor from hell begins to operate in free will of mind or starts to show signs of disengagement from his hell-family- regiment, the regimental-heads will use their invisible controlling powers to try to override such free will of choice and keep it locked on evil choices. The only will in operation in evil is evil and as such, an evil spirit is only in mind of evil and nothing else. To attempt to walk in free will is evidence of ability to choose good out of good and evil and if this were to happen, it means the spirit will no longer be under the evil will control of the evil-regiments. Once the regimental leader sees any signs of free will, they will immediately seek to cut-short the soul's time-era visit by orchestrating the mind to destroy the visible body by for instance: suicide.

The regimental-heads do not wish for any human in the world to choose the ways of God. This is mainly because they know that once a man finds God, his soul will be disengaged from the soul of the evil-regiment leader. As a result, darkness will no longer be able to rule and control his soul and spirit. The evil will of the regimental leaders is to bury every soul in the darkness-hell. As time travelers and wanderers, the regimental-heads have a time-era controlling and ruling aim to prevent humans from finding God. The invisible, principality-angels knowing that their time is up, seek to bring their hell-system of darkness fully to the surface of the earth—in order to place a total barrier of darkness between man and God.

The spiritual sea—which is symbolic of hell, is the largest, mysterious aspect of human life. Understanding of this mystery has to be by direct revelation from the Holy Spirit, not just by the black and white information. Without revelation it will be impossible to understand these things from a natural logic mindset. To have further revelation it is important to seek and develop a personal relationship with the God of the Bible with a humble heart so He can open the spiritual eyes to see and understand things for what they are.

Through God's revelations, I learnt in my soul that the true root of all human suffering is in the first Adam. When Adam sinned, he and his descendants became prisoners of time—to serve time with hard labour. Freedom from this hard labour comes only by choosing goodness out of good and evil. This choice is a choice that all descendants of the first Adam can only make in the physical, visible world. This is because once a spirit goes into invisible consciousness, they will see evil for what it is and as such can no longer change their mind to choose goodness. In the fall of Man, Adam and his descendants became subject to the darkness rule of the principality-angels.

However, whosoever chooses goodness on their visit to earth will no longer be subject to serving time in the prison-realm of the wicked fallen angels. The angels that fell from heaven are fully aware of God's grace for man and know for sure that God's predestined Day of Judgement is at hand. They are also aware that the visible Earth is the only place whereby the descendants of the first Adam can choose goodness. Choosing goodness between good (Christ) and evil (Satan) is the only way of reversing the Adamic curse, which came upon Adam and from Adam his entire human spiritual descendants. To debar man from making the all important spiritual choices that will set their souls free from this sinful curse, the wicked fallen angels in rotation order journeyed to the time-era in the dispensations of time to create many doors of confusion.

To place man in complete darkness of God's righteousness, the wicked angels aim to bring hell to the surface of the world in the final hours of the end-times. Under this hell-system, humans in the world will carry in their body tracking-devices and these tracking-devices will track their every bodily movement and project the image of their movements to the central world-commanding centre. This world tracking-device is not the same as a soul tracking-device and therefore it cannot track any soul that is already disengaged from the hell-system of darkness. However, the entire idea behind the visible tracking-device is to place humans fully under a system of extreme fear. Under this extreme watch system of fear, humans will only be in fear of the beastly-man and no longer in any fear of the real God. Without the fear of God, humans will have no wisdom and knowledge of God. Lacking real knowledge of God, humans will go deeper into the darkness-regime of fear of principality-heads of hell.

God opened my eyes to see the various principality-heads of the beastly-order as they journeyed from the spiritual sea to the world and the sea that they came from is: hell. In their real appearances, they looked like dragons but unable to spit fire. Instead of fire, they spit terrible smelling, dirty poisonous water into the souls of humans. All those that have this water in their souls are full of hatred for God. I saw that the world centre of hell is in the middle of the sea. The sea-heads of governors are warlords and they hide behind the faces of the various world rulers that are in the middle of the sea. The main head to the world government of the sea has in my time-era the face of a female. This female looking head has immense power in the spirit world of darkness sea-regiment and many are fearful and afraid of her. Many worship her as a goddess of the sea and she has had under her control for quite a long period much of the sea area. As a major ruler of darkness, many are under her controlling feet and they seek to please her to obtain territorial ruling powers from her.

When the Lord revealed the true face and colour behind the mask to me, this main head with a female looking face came after me to spiritually attack me, to try to place me in confusion of her real identity. However, the Lord shielded and protected me with His power and everything she did only worked to further reveal her hidden secrets to me. The various heads of principalities not only wish to rule the world, but also seek for humans to worship them—instead of God. I saw them journeying from the sea to the earth to erect various monuments of confusion, in order to place humans in dark mind of true-life worship. They uttered from their mouth many doctrines to sell unto humans, and whosoever purchased their doctrines is thereinafter marked with a special 'mark of the beast' as a worshiper of the beast. They came in many forms, shapes and sizes from one generation to the next to sell all kinds of doctrines and ideas unto humans so that humans would be far away from having real-knowledge of the true God. The main strategy of the heads of principalities in all aspects is deceitfulness.

They journey to earth in their many numbers to deceive humans and lead them far away from the one true God. Throughout time they have journeyed to the visible world in all shapes, colours, sizes and sexes to bring to the visible the darkness of the invisible hell. God revealed the principality-faces behind the various doctrines of the world and I saw that they are all associates of the beastly, fallen angel (Lucifer). I saw that many of the principality-heads are hiding in the bodies of the world rulers and world celebrities, and many of the creatures that are in the world of darkness worship them as gods and goddesses. Consequently they are not able to see the perfect image of the Morning Star Jesus Christ (2 Peter 1:19,

Revelation 22:16).

The principality-heads have erected several sinful images for humans to idolise in the world and with the humans fixated upon their ungodly idols; they deny themselves the sight of God's own perfect image of redemption. The principality-angels are traders of death from the sea-world of hell. Their main marketing aim is to cunningly package sinful rebellion and deceive humans to purchase it as an attractive product of enjoyment, hence, preventing them from receiving the grace of God. They created different kinds of unholy world temples and misled humans to establish all manner of movements to confuse the masses from one generation to another. In their several journeys to Earth, they have succeeded in selling to humans all kinds of principality doctrines to blindfold them from seeing the true-life principles of God. These doctrines are many and several in number and close to judgement day, many more doctrines from the principality- heads will be brought to the visible surface of the world. This is to deceive man—mainly to bury their souls deeper in darkness-principality rule.

One of their major doctrines already bought by many in the world is that God does not exist and that it is a mythical superstitious idea to say that there is God and that He created the heavens and the earth. This doctrine not only denies the existence of God but goes on to suggest an alternative idea to Creation by God; which is that the earth evolved all on its' own and as such will dissolve on its own. Another one of many such doctrines claims that not one God created the heavens and earth but many 'gods' As such, so long as a human being chooses one of the many heads of creation, he or she will be deemed to be serving all creational heads of the galaxy via their chosen route. The main objective behind the open propagation of these false doctrines and ideas is to prevent humans from discovering their true roots.

Just as the principality-angels journeyed in time to earth in their many numbers, to confuse man with various false doctrines, God also as the only Head that is above all principalities and powers journeyed from His invisible existence into the visible world to make clear the only true doctrine. God did not journey from the invisible to the visible for world-ruling aims or purposes. God came once and for all to place humans in the blessings of His Immortal existence and He will return on the last day of time to dispense final judgement to the world of sin. God as a Holy God has no reason for coming to the world for any kind of worldly agenda. This is because the real world and kingdom of life that God wants humans to see is His invisible eternal life kingdom of light.

God is above all principalities and powers and as the overall ruler in all dominion and dimensional realms, He has controlling power over and above all. To be visible is to be a mortal and God as the Head that is above all principalities and powers is the invisible and immortal Triune One God, everlastingly. God does not intend to abandon His eternal kingdom abode at any time or era, just to come and rule an ugly world of sin. Instead, God came to open the eyes of humans to see His real kingdom of peace, joy and rest. God's kingdom is His throne-land and as His throne-land, always full of His Glory. God has set the world of sin aside to be a regeneration ground for the soul of man and once His predestined era of regeneration runs its course, God intends to destroy the world of sin together with the entire wicked souls that are in it.

God came from His invisible eternal life-realm to the earthly mortal world, purposely to make His universal ruling order of 'light' visible to man as love. To enable man to be a partaker of His universal kingdom of light and goodness, God came and gave His flesh and blood so that by choosing God's own flesh and blood, man would have chosen Him as entire goodness and as such would no longer be subject to the evil curses of darkness rulers. God's flesh and blood revealed in the Person is Christ Jesus and whosoever spiritually eats of His flesh and drinks of His blood will acquire the Spirit, heart, body and mind of God. Those that have the Spirit, heart, body and mind of God will have a soul-to-soul connection with God. In their soul connection with God, they would come under the loving ruling-system of God's eternal life and Holy Kingdom and as such, they would no longer live in fear of death. This is the only true doctrine, hence hell and its principality-angels knowing this to be the only Truth, work tirelessly to prevent every spirit of mankind from finding this Truth in the world.

The hellish deceivers are skilled in their deceitful ways and they deceive humans from generation to generation with fake alternatives to God's true doctrine of salvation. God opened my eyes to see that they have bastardised everything, especially the church arena so that humans do not connect to the true ways of God that He has established within His real church. The heads of principalities are the first and last universal prisoners. However, even in their hell-prison-yard, they desire to rule humans that became their co-prisoners and associates after falling from the light-ruling regiment of God into the sinful order of death. The darkness system of the principality-angels is a system of fear. They deceive man to submit to their ways of darkness rule by promoting fear of death in the visible world. Through instilling fear in the mind, they rule the mind of many who submit to their ways due to fear of death. Some willingly submit themselves unto the deadly dark ruling forces, because they think they are doing God a favour, while others offer themselves to death because they could not see any hope of life at all from the world of darkness.

The wicked spirits of hell hide their faces behind the natural faces of humans. They control humans from the inside by leading them to create havoc and chaos in the world. They control the minds of humans to purchase and propagate a sinful order, so that human beings in sinful order remain subject to their principality darkness rule. Every soul that connects to the principality-heads of hell carries a unique mark that identifies them with the regiment they belong to. Some belong to the regiments of witchcraft. Others belong to the heads of regiment of the sea-world. There are also those that belong to a soldiery regiment. The world spirits that are from the soldiery regiment have in addition to their normal beastly mark a special mark that identifies them as soldiers of hell. Demonic warlords that are very hungry for human flesh and thirsty for human blood occupy those that carry the special soldiery mark of the beast. These warlords are cosmos super intelligent skilled aliens and human-hunters. Each warlord is in control of uncountable battalions of hell's demonic soldiers. God opened my eyes to see that principality-angels as prisoners of hell are time travellers and until the hands of the clock in the era of time stops, they will continue to journey back and forth the sea-world of darkness.

The main end-time aim of the fallen angels is to devalue humans altogether and replace them with human-sized, special killer robotic machines. These will be programmed to do evil and humans will not be able to resist being hunted down and fed to the evil principality-angels as food. This evil 'robotic plan' is already in progress. The principality aliens have already programmed many humans on the inside to be their killer specimen machine-robots in the outside world. These human robotic killer machines are only interested in preying on other human beings, make their lives full of misery and ultimately hunt them down and feed them to their alien taskmasters. I saw many programmed human specimen robots walking around the earth globe marching to the commandments of their alien taskmaster to prey on and hunt down fellow humans. They appeared as ordinary humans on the outside, but locked within the human body is the ugly body and killing will of robotic killer alien soldiers of hell.

The bodies occupied by the soldiers of hell work tirelessly to bring the sea's wicked order of death to the surface of the world—to place the whole world in darkness of the true God. They feed the human minds with all kinds of iniquity ideas. They focus human minds on the sky to receive false signs and doctrines from the beast. Those that focus their eyes on the sky for signs cannot see the real signs from heaven. As a result, the world's beastly-order continues to dominate their minds and souls.

The entire world's beastly-order is heavily into mind games and these mind games are gambling games of evil cards. Their joker card on humans begins with 6 and ends with 6. They deceive humans from the inside in order to keep them engaged in their evil games, so that with the human busy playing the cards of losers, they will not see the heart and true glory of God. It is only when humans have the card number 777 that they will win the game and the One that holds all the sevens is Christ Jesus, the Master of the game. Whosoever has all the sevens will see that the joke is already on the wicked enemy. But whosoever continues to play the game of sixes will continue to walk in condemnation of the wicked joker player.

The beastly soldier-animals of hell are everywhere and their own game is spiritual Russian roulette. They stir up violent passions in humans to engage them in a violent spiritual game of Russian roulette and feed their minds with hatred towards each other. They regulate and program the human mind to be mindful of killing their fellow human counterparts and deceive them to believe that they are winning the game of life by their killing each other. They blindfold the eyes of humans with many false ideas and lead them to have extreme hatred for each other. They train and program many to be killer weapons, so that from the many killings they will have plenty of food supply. With the wicked enemy soldiers lurking in the body of humans, many in the world are walking around and looking like free people when actually they are prisoners of war of the hell soldiers.

No human in the world is an island. Every soul has a connection to a soul, and every soul operates in the objective mind of their soul's regiment. Those connected to the magic and witchcraft regiments for example, derive inspiration from their magic and witchcraft regiments to sell magic and witchcraft ideas to the world. I saw that most spirits in the world are in soul connection with dark regiments of principalities. Therefore, most spirits of the world are the 'walking living dead' and as the 'walking dead', they are sorrowfully evil and wicked. The walking dead are subject to all kinds of abuse and attacks from their demonic companions and due to this, always deeply sorrowful in their minds.

The defence and protection against the attack of darkness abuse is the light shield and cover from God, and the only way for any human to acquire this light shield of protection is to give their soul, body and mind to Christ Jesus. With so much confusion in the world, many are antichrist and as antichrists, walk round the earth without Christ's protective light. I saw demons go in and out of the many defenceless human bodies. Some have battalions of hell soldiers following them around and in bad company of hell soldiers they have no mind to purchase the Truth of Christ that came from heaven. The creatures from hell are very ugly and they smell terribly. I saw that the world cults and groups serve as secret hiding places for many and the members of the various cults guard their cult's secrets with everything possible. Whosoever joins the cults must swear a secret oath vowing never to divulge the secret operations of the cult. The cults will deal mercilessly with anyone that in any way breaches the oath of keeping the cult's secrets operations secret.

God opened my eyes to see the cult-regiments that are in all corners of the world. I saw that there are different types of cults, ranging from low-level to top-level, and I saw that most of the world's prominent faces are secret cult members. God opened my eyes to see the top-level cults and revealed faces of their various members to me. I saw that various heads of world governments are prominent members of these cults. I saw that most heads of government that are in the mid-centre of the sea hold prominent and key positions in the top-level world cults.

The rulers of darkness in the mid-centre of the sea are the central poisonous tail of the beast, and their main role is to bring the beastly poison in them to the surface of the world's centre and from there spread it across the globe. The World Order as the darkness 'tail order' of the beast aspires to promote a godless and unholy society. It seeks to focus the minds of people on lustful pursuit of self-righteousness. The main objective of their central commanding order is to pave the way for the establishment of a global sea-world, principality order government. In this sea-world principality government order, humans will live in greater fear of the principality-angels and as such, will have deeper hatred for God. Without the fear of God, the world of humans will be a world of greater sorrow, oppression, madness and depression.

God further opened my eyes to see the state of the world nearer to the last days of God's judgement. I saw that all principality-heads of governments came from the sea to rule the world. The last to come out of the sea to the surface of the earth will be the 'beast'. In the last hour of time, the beast, by joining his head with entire principality-head will dispense greater evil from its human tail to sting the entire world than ever before seen or recorded in the history of mankind. This beast came in the body of a man, pretending to be a peacemaker, but he had no mind of peace whatsoever, because he will be in unity with the beast as the beast. The human beast will pretend to be a peacemaker and will have the power of the adjoining three heads of the beast. The three adjoining heads of the beast each represent sin, self-righteousness and death. The beast from the sea will give the power from his beastly head to the seven tails of the beast in order to poison the entire world with deep rulings of darkness. He will place the mind of the whole world in greater fear of terror and make many to accept the 'mark of the beast'.

Humans in fear and terror of the beast will submit their will to the beast, and by so doing give power to the entire head and body of the beast to rule and terrorise them from his cage prison. Although the dead beast had no powers to free itself from its abyss' cage prison, yet appeared to be able to exercise extreme powers through its evil human World Order poisonous tail. Although dead and without powers—the beast, by joining its heads with Man, ruled from the soul of the fallen man as its main head. The beast terrorised man with much greater wickedness from the human World Order poisonous tail. The World Order ruling flesh of the beast marked those that worshipped the beast with the 'Beastly Mark'. Those that worshipped the beast were slaves of darkness and as slaves of darkness; they readily yielded to every evil order of the beast.

I saw the visible image of the beast terrorise all humans across the globe and place a tracking-device on all newborn babies. He brought hell to the entire surface of the world and the world was in deep sorrow and hellish darkness. He used humans as guinea pigs and programmed their minds to be completely antichrist, just as he is. He spoke evil words of blasphemy and sorrow of death was deeply everywhere in the world. I saw that the world was in deep darkness and masses of humans under the beastly-order lacked true knowledge of God.

In fear of the world's beastly government order, they willingly received the tracking mark of the beast and with this mark they were crippled by greater fear. I saw human-sized robot soldiers everywhere. They were programmed to kill humans for fun and games. With many of these robot soldiers walked around in the world, the walking spiritually dead human lived in fear of death. And in fear of death they walked in the opposite of God's own righteous order. In deep fear many had permanently removed themselves from the divine, peaceful, and righteous loving ruling order of the Trinity, One God.

I saw a final end-time world that had undergone so much destruction, beyond recognition. I saw different kinds of strange looking humans. Some were half-animal and half-human. Others looked like half-machine and half-human programmed to kill the real humans and give them as food to the principality-angels. I saw many faces of humans that were suffering different kinds of economic depression and oppression. I saw a ground zero world of chaotic disorder in which there was no value and respect for humans.

In this extreme last hour evil world, humans were no longer valued resources or assets. This was mainly because the human-sized robots were the ones performing the everyday tasks and roles that the real humans perform in today's world. I saw many humans that were starving and hiding from the human-sized robotic killer machines. I saw a world of great darkness and wickedness, full of flesh eating and blood drinking barbarians. The only thing in the minds of those that were in the high places of the world was extreme wickedness and most humans were in great sorrow.

I saw a world whereby many no longer believed in Christ or in His return to judge the world. The congregation of humans under the order of hell had become totally antichrist and the beastly World Order dealt mercilessly with anyone that sought to promote the 'goodness' Name of Christ. The spiritually dead human body of the beast, which is the tail of the beast, believed it had travelled and seen every place in the galaxy. It thought it had the entire universe under its control to do as it pleased without any responsibility or accountability to anyone, but itself. Humans in the world were only in mind of sodomy and were full of harlotry and evil sexual desires that are against the will of God.

In sight of these things, I was deeply heavy hearted. God however made me to understand that all of these things only occurred for prophetic fulfilment purposes, so that everyone in all realms bear witness and record of fulfilment to all true prophesies. Also, that they came to pass as they were written and predestined to be fulfilled. In line with His record of prophetic fulfilment, God opened my eyes to see that at a time when humans are overly drunk with evil power, in deafness to God's Word and in complete wickedness of mind, He the God of the universe puts an end to the beastly world-era of sin.

I saw Him call every spirit unto judgement, as it is written. Then He affirmed eternal life as the reward for the saints and eternal death for the spirits of darkness. Subsequently, He ordered the angels to throw the beast and his wicked associates into the lake of fire. Finally, He commanded fire to rain upon the earth and the world and the sea passed away and was no more. God condemned the sea and all spirits of the sea-world to perish forever in the eternal lake of fire. Following this final condemnation, God closed the gate of death and shut the door to the realm of death forever so that no spirit of death would ever again be able to travel from the realm of death to anywhere in the universe. Never again in the universe of life would there be sea or any spirits of the sea following God's closure and His sealing of the gateway to and from the realm of the spiritual sea and darkness. At the passing away of the old earth, which had the sea as hell in its centre, God opened the gate of eternal life in a new heaven and earth to all the saints and there was no more sea in this new heaven and new earth.

After what seemed like many years of driving around and what appeared to be endless revelations, we headed back home. However it wasn't long after we got home that I found myself handcuffed, forced into an ambulance headed for a mental health hospital.

CHAPTER SEVEN
THE JUNCTION OF FINAL FRONTIER

"I will bless the LORD, who hath given me counsel: my reins also instruct me in the night seasons. I have set the LORD always before me: because he is at my right hand, I shall not be moved. Therefore my heart is glad, and my glory rejoiceth: my flesh also shall rest in hope. For thou wilt not leave my soul in hell; neither wilt thou suffer thine Holy One to see corruption. Thou wilt show me the path of life: in thy presence is fulness of joy; at thy right hand there are pleasures forevermore".

—Psalm 16: 7-11

All I wanted to do when we arrived back home was to just sit down and deliberate on all the things that I had seen thus far. I sat on one of our living room chairs hoping for a bit of relaxation. However, it wasn't long before I found myself engaged in another round of fierce battle. In the midst of my unending battle, I continued seeing all manner of weird images and the counting and humming sound that I had heard when we were out for a drive, became much louder than it had been when I was outside the house. I began pacing up and down again due to the continuation of my overwhelming experience. Deep into my battle and revelation experiences, I heard the voice of the Lord Jesus say:

Your victory is a gift from Me and it is established in the dominion of light everlastingly. I, as the supreme Head ruler of the universe gave you your victory and every authority and power in all dominion realms will acknowledge and recognise the authority in you as supreme. Now with boldness of faith you must declare your victory and fully operate in the supreme authority that is in you in all dominions and dimensional realms. Arise now, go and operate in the victory authority that is in you in all visible and invisible realms of: sound, fire, sea, and ocean, air, in all realms beneath the earth, above the sky and in all flesh territorial realms of darkness.

The moment He finished speaking His words to me, I suddenly became conscious of the fact that the television in the living room was actually on and for some reason I felt compelled to watch it. So I sat down. The first thing I noticed as I sat down to watch was that the television set no longer appeared as the usual image transmission box. Instead it seemed more like some hypnotic communication channel used by alien spirits to transmit messages of death into the hearts and minds of people. I realised that what the ordinary eyes see on the television set is quite different from what actually goes on in the invisible channel waves.

From the ordinary eye perspective, the television images appear as mere entertainment, good fun and harmless information. However from the invisible eye perspective, I realised that behind what seemed like harmless transmissions of entertainment and information were deadly hypnotic coded messages. With my spiritual eyes now wide open, I was able to see the hidden alien beings that are behind the human mask, busy transmitting their hypnotic coded messages from the channel waves of the TV box direct into the viewers mind. They communicated in some sign language and I heard the Lord say, "Pay attention to their hand signals and you will begin to understand their channel signals".

The moment I focused on the hand signals in line with the Lord's instruction, I began to see that what the natural mouth was saying was actually the opposite of what the hands were signalling. From their mouth came words that sounded harmless, but their hands were signalling something completely different. Their hands were signalling and discharging terrible, deadly messages whilst their mouth spoke what sounded like wonderful, good fun. The signals from the hands seemed to have some kind of hypnotic effect, which turns the viewer into an addict that will continually yearn for more of the poisonous messages coming from the television spiritual channel waves. The picture looked harmless, but the hand signals behind the picture transmitted terrible and wicked messages directly into people's minds. No ordinary eyes could see the signals or understand the poisonous effects from them.

The Lord further opened my eyes to understand the coded messages from their hand signals. I began to see that they frequently blasphemed with their mouth and repeatedly signalled with their hands, that it was over for the beast, but that many souls were going down with him to the pit. From my being able to understand their hand signals, I was able to decode the hidden messages they were transmitting from their various death- medium and channel waves. I saw their hands continually signalling the following messages:

We can see you all, but you can never see us. Although you all think you can see, you see nothing because you are all blind and deaf. We are hiding inside you to destroy you from your within. We've come to shatter your world and mislead you to destroy one another. You are our food and we will feed on your flesh. We will make your women harlots and shall corrupt your men to only be mindful of sodomy. We will make you evil predators to prey on your own children, and you cannot escape us because we rule your minds from your within. We will trouble your minds and you shall not have peace or rest.

We will take your children and turn them against you. We've come to prevent your children from finding the glory of life. We will poison their souls with the serpent's lust for violence and evil. We will lead their minds to enjoy and love violence and hate peace. They will be addicted to sin and we will keep them engaged in evil deeds and focus their minds on us. We will destroy their minds with drugs and we will make them useless through liquor. We have fashioned a path of destruction for them and they will follow this path without any remorse. They will see us as their heroes and role models and they will be addicted to emulating us. They will not listen to the Truth and they will hate righteousness. We have come to prepare your minds for extreme evil and wickedness. Hell is come to you O world of flesh.

As I began to decode their hand signals through the Lord's power of revelations, the Lord made me to further realise that the poisonous words from the signals were not just mere expressions or threats, but sinful commandments from the alien which has a terrible hypnotic and addictive effect on the mind of the receiver. I continued to see their hands signalling further sinful commandments, all for the purpose of hardening the hearts and minds of the receiver to remain a partaker of their sinful condemnation. I also saw their hands signalling:

You will all be addicted to sin and you will not be able to stop yourselves from sinning. Sinfulness will be your desire and you must consider it your right to sin. You must walk in disobedience and you must love the world and the things of the world. Stay blind for we do not want you to see. We are in your mind in order to lead you to self-destruct yourselves from your within. Sinning will be your only desire. Go and perform evil deeds to feed your lust for wickedness. Receive the poison of the beast and be wicked. Be depressed and be evil minded. Be rebellious and hate one another. Kill one another and be evil and wicked to each other. Hate God and love Satan. Deny Christ and walk in mind of the antichrist. Be promiscuous and lustful.

Go and chase after worldly things and do not listen to the Truth. Be ungodly and be confused. Enjoy sin and pursue it as your right. Be murderers, thieves, and harlots and be angry with God. Seek world fame and chase vanity. These commandments you must follow. Now go and fulfil them as we command you.

The Lord gave me understanding to see that many receive these sinful commandments daily and with no power to resist, they follow them to their destructive ends. The Lord opened my eyes further to see the hidden results of their hypnotic sinful commandments. I saw a world full of people obsessed with violence and promiscuity because they had no power to resist the wicked commandments. With several humans buried under the wicked hypnotic-spell of the evil demonic spirits, the world was full of many with hearts of rebellion against God. I saw a picture of increased violence in the final hours of the end-time and many were in painful sorrow.

As I continued to watch these revelation images, I suddenly saw a picture of myself—sitting and watching television the way I used to before the start of my encounter in 2003. I saw myself concentrating on watching what seemed then as entertainment and saw the alien spirits signalling from the screen saying:

Be frustrated and depressed. Go and kill yourself. Go and be lustful. Love the world and chase after the things of the world. Hate God and love sin. There is a glory on your head but you can never find it because you are blind and cannot see.

I saw myself totally hypnotised to lust after the things of the flesh. However, I also saw that whilst they were busy hypnotising my mind to sin, Christ had worked everything out to bring me the signal of joy. Following the display of several pictures of my past hypnotic television viewing sessions, I saw myself seated as I had sat in October 2003. I saw a signal of light beaming on my face as I listened to the In Touch Ministries preacher's message. I saw my spirit leap for joy after receiving the light signal and saw that ever since then, I had power of resistance and discernment operating in me which enables me to immediately reject the poisonous expressions and evil commandments. With my spirit in awakening of light, my flesh became dead to sin and I no longer had the sinful lust and urge to continue walking in sin, no matter how strong their signal got.

I then saw that all flesh had been against me from the moment I acquired my spiritual light signal and power to reject the evil commands from the channels of death. I saw that all flesh was against me in order to prevent me from having a conscious understanding of the Power and Truth of Christ in me. Though invisible to my eyes then, I was now able to see that from the moment I had received my spiritual light signal, Christ had actually been there standing by my side helping me with His power of light to resist the alien evil commandments. I saw that the aliens had been busy signalling to me from their channel waves previous to the start of my revelation experience that my hour of great temptation had come. However, since my spiritual eyes were not, as of then open for me to clearly see their signal messages for what it was, I had no way of understanding what they were signalling to me. I remembered there was a time we had a terrible interruption with our television set and from then on, it stopped working.

I also remembered seeing a cloud shape of the Cross directly above my house around the month of April 2004, but as at that time I had no idea why and I did not pay any attention to it in my mind. With my spiritual eyes now wide open, the Lord enabled me to see and understand that the interruption with the television wasn't an ordinary interruption but a strong signal from the channel wave of death that my hour of great temptation was around the corner. The Lord also made me to understand that the shape of the cross that I had seen above my house had not been a figure of my imagination, but had actually been a signal from Him to reassure me that I have His grace of victory. And that by His grace, even though I was due to be tried, I would surely testify to His Resurrection and partake in His eternal victory over death.

Having clarified this to my mind, God fast-forwarded my

revelation experience and once again concentrated my attention on the current signals coming from my no longer, natural looking television transmission box. God at this point further opened my eyes to see the faces behind the signals. I saw that the various signals came from the principality-heads and their faces were now visible to me and not at all hidden. I saw that they all have cunningly erected various evil monuments and wicked 'media-wave' channels as their synagogues of sin. Also, I could see them discharging their coded messages of sin (from their secret hiding places) to their unsuspecting world congregations. I saw that they had countless followers like sea sand, who were highly committed to spreading their sinful messages to the world. They had a terrible desperate look of destruction in their eyes and they were extremely ugly in appearance.

Hidden Agenda of the Media Wave of Evil Revealed

As I continued to watch, I suddenly realised that they were now directing their signalling messages specifically at me. I saw their hands signalling to me and they began revealing their evil media-wave agenda in the following wicked signalling sayings:

Now that you have seen what you are not meant to see and have heard what you are not meant to hear, you will never be a normal being in the natural world unless you join us, for to see us is to run mad. No one sees the secret of evil at the extent that you have seen it and lives to testify against us. To know the secret of evil and choose not to join hands with evil is against the total spiritual order of life. Whether good or evil all secrets are revealed by God for God's glory. You walk in the full glory of God when you join hands with evil in order to achieve entire life's purpose in the natural world. If you refuse to join us we have permission from God to toy with your mind and play with your head and we will certify you as mad in the natural world. Now you know the Truth of Christ and have seen the glory upon your head. However as for that glory upon your head, we will never allow it to shine forth for the world to see, unless you join us and by so doing keep our secrets to yourself. If you choose to reveal our secrets, then we will cause illusion to rule your mind.

To see the total hidden secret of the spirit in your natural existence is to pay a heavy price with your natural life, and this price is madness in the world. We know you are victorious in the invisible and we can never dispute that. However what is the use of your victory if you fail to declare it in the only place that counts most. The spirit knows the spirit so the identity of a spirit being is clearly visible to the spiritual eyes of another spirit being. However the secret of life in the visible is that no human should know his own identity let alone that of another.

The outer flesh of humans covers the real spiritual identity of the spirit hibernating within the cover of the flesh. Unless a human being is prepared to enter into a conscious relationship with the hidden spirit that is on the inside and by so doing, keep the identity secret—the identity of the spirit on the inside will remain hidden. Good and evil are hidden secrets of life and God has not revealed our identity to you, so that you will reveal it to the world in the manner that you are planning to in your heart. Instead, He revealed our identity to you for you to join us to work together for His glory.

God's plan and aim is for all secrets of good and evil to remain secret for Him to secretly work it all together in His power for His glory. We know that your mission is to go into the world and testify to Truth of the Saviour, which you have seen to the glory of God the Creator. However, we have built a barrier of unbelief in the minds of humans to make your mission impossible. You will only be on record as a spirit that fulfilled all her life's missions and objectives if you succeed in serving your entire spiritual purpose in all dominion and dimensional realms of life and death.

You have declared your victory in the spirit-realm and we admit you have won in the spirit-realm but with the help of God of course. However you have heard from the Creator Himself that to be an all around winner, you must overcome your natural fears just as you have overcome your spiritual fears and it is with our help only, that you can overcome all your natural fears.

Your natural fear is madness and how can you have the faith to declare the Truth of Jesus in the madness of your own fears? Your only chance is to join us. If you join us we will not oppose you or scare your mind into deep madness. We will back you with fake miracles and make many to believe in you and to follow you as your disciples. You will be very rich and you will be able to influence the world as you please. Everything will still work out for the glory of God, because your message will still be of Christ Jesus as the Son of God. We will not oppose you in preaching the Gospel of Jesus Christ.

All we ask is that you do this by joining hands with us and everything shall work out to your advantage both in the invisible spirit-realm and in the natural world. We will help you spread the Word of the Gospel by making you a world famous star and many shall come from all corners of the world to hear your Christ message and watch you perform many miracles. With our helping hand you will bring many souls to God and God will highly reward you for making such a huge impact in the world. Your legacy will be monumental and the whole world will continue to speak of all that you have done in the Name of God till the end of days.

However, if you are against us you will not be able to make such impact, for we have control of the natural and have God's permission to direct everything in time to achieve any kind of natural results that pleases us. If you will join hands with us and not divulge our major secrets, you will serve your mission in life full of total power and everyday enjoyment in the natural world. You have nothing to lose because when you finally take your leave from the natural world, you will continue to enjoy your God given spiritual victory in the invisible spirit-realm forever. God has permanently given you your spiritual victory and no matter what you do, He will never take your victory from you because He is always faithful to His Word. Only thing is that He cannot help you to achieve the natural results that your heart so much desires and He also desires for you to achieve.

God controls the supernatural and He expects you to take

141

control in the natural by your own free will of choice and what brings results in the natural is evil not good. Evil in the natural works for supernatural good, hence you cannot do without us because it is only if you join hands with us that you shall achieve all of your natural aims for the supernatural glory of God. If you want natural results, you must join hands with us for we are also working for the glory of God. Have you not heard of the Scripture that says good and evil shall work together for those that love God given that He foreknew and predestined them to fulfil His glorious purpose? This is a true and factual Scripture and God expects you to choose in mind of the wisdom Words that are in the Scriptures. God Himself uses evil to achieve good, for to get positive results you cannot do without the negative.

Even Christ who you believe in, was it not the hands of evil that crucified Him? Had He not been crucified by the hands of evil, there would have been no gospel. You need us and we need you, so why not let us work together for the glory of God? It is only when you make use of good and evil that you will achieve a total good end result—both in the spirit and in the natural. This is your God given aim, to achieve total goodness through proper utilisation of our evil powers. It is wise for you to take the services that we are offering you and use it to achieve all your godly aims. Without our help, it is impossible for you to fulfil your life missions on earth, for it is only through evil assistance that you can fulfil your life's aims in the natural.

God has given us control over everything in the natural and if you join us, you will have all your worldly desires. When it comes to natural results, God expects you to achieve it by joining hands with evil and although He is for you in the spirit-realm, He will forsake you in the natural if you fail to do the wise thing, which is to join hands with evil in the natural. We are committed to giving natural results that will bring continuous joy to your heart and we will not abandon you. You have God's full spiritual support so, irrespective of your natural choices, you are an already all round winner. God is the authority over both good and evil and He wants you to utilise our evil powers for goodness sake. He will not rebuke you for doing what is right, which is for you to use evil to obtain good results.

If however you fail to listen to the voice of reason, from now on all your fellow human beings shall see you as mad and no one will believe you. The world is only interested in believing when they have seen and what your eyes have seen no one sees and humans do not believe in what the ordinary eyes cannot see. How will that serve God's purpose on earth if you appear mad in the eyes of those you want to preach the message of hope and life to? You must be sane in the eyes of humans for you to make the impact God wants you to make in the natural world. It is only with our help that you will walk in total faithfulness to God. God expects you to use evil to achieve good and if you fail to do just that, then you will end up spending your time on earth not fulfilling your entire godly aims of making a global impact.

Although God will not take your spiritual victory from you

because He is true to His Words, He will demote you in the spirit-realm for choosing wrongly in the natural. Is this what you want? If you refuse to join us, then your spiritual belief shall only work to make you appear mad in the natural and God cannot help you overcome your fears in the natural as He did for you in the spirit-realm. Without natural help from God you will not be able to do this on your own, unless you accept our offer to help you. We have absolute control in the natural and God Himself gave us the control that we have to direct the hands of time and to bring a kind of timely result, which will propel you to immediate success in the natural. We guarantee you immediate success, so why prolong your success when it is at your fingertips? All you have to do is say, 'Yes' to keeping our major secrets secret, and immediately you will begin to experience a continuous chain reaction of breakthroughs in the natural world.

Success in the natural world, just as you have it in the spiritual world is what you want, is it not? Well, that is exactly all you will have from us. We will give you a world of success that no ordinary eyes have seen before and you will enjoy it for the rest of your stay in time without any interruption from failure. We know that you love God and we are sure He loves you and surely you are in no mind to betray the One you love and we will never encourage you to do so. Instead, all we are asking is that you keep our main secret safe as God Himself intends for you to, and you will soon begin to enjoy the best of both worlds. God intends for the secret of evil to remain secret for He does not want the whole world to know the secret of evil, so that life on earth would still be fun and games full of challenges for humans.

God knows humans enjoy the challenges of the natural world and He intends to keep them busy with increasing ongoing challenges. This is so that when they finally overcome, they will glorify Him. We know God for we were with Him before the foundation of the world and we know that He created all things both good and evil for sake of His glory. He has kept the secret of good and evil from humans so that they would glorify Him as the All in all when He reveals it to them individually, in His own time. He appointed this time to reveal all secrets to you, not for you to reveal it to the whole world and spoil human's fun and games, but to keep it safe within yourself and Glorify Him within you. He will reveal secrets to individuals in His own appointed time and that way, life on earth will continue to be a mystery to humans all for the glory of God. If you join hands with us, you will continue to enjoy an open world of secrets in the presence of the invisible God and you will live the rest of your life on earth in a world of godly riches.

In the world of flesh, we control the mind, the body and the hearts. We have power to confuse the minds and render a spirit insane. The world is a home of dark spirits and we have control over all spirits of darkness that are in the world. The human flesh yields to our commandments without resistance and we will make all flesh work to your glory and for the glory of the God that you believe in. You will enjoy continuous promotions in the world and we will give you control over many legions of dark spirits. They will all work to bring you the kind results you desire to have. We can make people believe you by backing you with fake miracles.

We will help you by ensuring that everyone that comes to you ends up with their heart's desires and that way they will have no choice other than to believe in your powers and follow you as a disciple. We will assist you to have a huge global impact all the days of your life by ensuring that your ministry continues to have global world dominance and world popularity. We will help you achieve all that God promised that you will achieve in your lifetime in the natural world most especially global fame, territorial control, influence, affluence and great wealth.

However if you choose to be foolish and not join us, you will walk in fear and not faith and your fear shall be a growing madness in you. The more you try to speak of the things you have seen, the more the world will see you as mad and by seeing you as mad, they will disbelieve you and in their disbelieve, they will frustrate you. You cannot make the unbelievable, believable without our help because we are the rulers of darkness and we have the whole world in the palm of our hands. For your information an ambulance is due to depart from us to take you to a mental ward, which will be your permanent residence if you choose wrongly. God wants you to choose rightly hence, He has allowed us to give you another chance to choose to join us. He wants you to join us and make use of our services for the glory of His name. If you fail to choose rightly, He has given us permission to punish you in the natural to our heart's content and when it comes to contentment concerning evil deeds, we have none. If you refuse to join us, you will suffer all your life for nothing when you could actually spend the rest of your life enjoying the riches of the earth. After all it is written: "The earth is of the Lord's, the world and all that is in it". It is true the earth is the Lord's but note, that He has given us permission to distribute the things of this world for His glory sake.

He has given us the keys to world's wealth and also the power to distribute it to whosoever chooses wisely. If you join hands with us, you will automatically receive from us immeasurable wealth that will enable you have the kind of overall global impact God wants you to have. The rule of the game in the natural is different from the spiritual because unlike the spiritual realm, God is not visibly here to help you. And forget about the angels helping you because an angel will only rise to the tone of God's command and order. When it comes to natural decisions, an angel cannot help you to decide nor will God interfere, because He has given you a free will and interfering with your free will is against His rule of life. This is something you must do yourself and this is a decision you must make yourself without God's help. All you have to do to have what is rightly due to you is to choose wisely. To reject our hands is to trade world success for world failure. This is not the Will of God for you.

You cannot have dominion without robust financial means and if you reject us, you will be rejecting money. We own money and to have world dominion you must have money. Money is a necessary thing for you to have in the world and it is within our control. If you join hands with us, we will release the spirit of money to serve you with abundance and with so much money; you can perform your entire godly task in total natural convenience.

We want to be your friend not your enemy and if you reject our hands, you will face so much unnecessary hardships. What is the point of being our enemy when we can be friends? What is the use of suffering when you do not have to? This is your last chance to make the right choice as God intends for you to. As already mentioned, the ambulance is on its way to take you to a mental ward, if you are foolish enough to turn down our hands of friendship. However if you choose wisely and join us, we will stop the ambulance from coming your way and you can continue to live your normal life full of wealth and riches. By joining us, you will have the best of both worlds. You will enjoy the natural world to the fullest and when you finally leave, you will enjoy your spiritual victory in the highest promotions forever. As for us, you have seen the end but for you, you have a chance to enjoy life to the fullest in all realms and dominion. Be wise, take this opportunity and you will have a perfect record of victory and dominance in all dominion and dimensional realms.

As soon as they finished speaking these words, I began hearing a loud deafening, 'Join us, join us, join us' chant and it was as if all the spirits of hell were now just repeatedly, loudly saying, 'Join us' in one accord. From all I had heard and seen so far, I became totally convinced that not only are hell spirits desperately evil and wicked, they are unrepentantly determined on tempting and deceiving every human being to the end of days. As far as I was concerned, I had seen and heard enough and all I wanted to do at this point was to physically run back to heaven. Without further delay, I jumped up from my sit, grabbed my bag with the hope of making a run for it back into heaven. The moment I made it outside the house, I went straight for the car and locked myself in there. It wasn't long before I realised that locking myself inside the car wasn't the solution because the moment I locked the car doors, the deafening, 'Join us, join us, join us' chant became so unbearably loud in my ears. It was as if all hell spirits had followed me inside the car and I felt totally trapped without any form of idea on how to escape back to my normal life. I had seen more than I could bear and all I wanted at this stage was to exit the world promptly and make my way back to heaven where I would be safe forever.

To escape what was now obvious to me as hell on earth, I decided to start the car engine and drive away into thin air and from there back to heaven. I was glad to hear the sound of the car engine. However, I did not move more than a few yards when suddenly the car engine stopped. I jumped out of the car the moment the car engine stopped and decided to make a run for it on foot. Everything in the world at this point including the car, my shoes and clothing now seemed to be chanting, 'Join us, join us'. I felt like stripping anything and everything of this world off my body. I even wanted my very own visible body to disappear into invisibility. I kicked off my shoes and started running as fast as I could even though I had no idea where I was actually headed. I thank God to this day for helping me keep my clothes on because everything at that moment felt as if it had been contaminated by evil.

As I kept running I could see countless hell spirits in pursuit and I saw no one on my side from the world of flesh. I saw all flesh—both dead and the living dead invisibly pursuing me in the visible world with desperate determination in their eyes to destroy me. I was able to identify each flesh for who they are and as I began mentioning them by their world names, I appeared as mad to the ordinary eyes because no ordinary eyes could witness what was going on. I wanted to be away from all flesh because no one looked human or appeared to be demonstrating normal human behaviours any longer and none was friendly toward me. I was determined more than ever to escape back to heaven and never again have anything to do with the world. Having realised that the evil plot of the wicked was to eradicate me, and every ounce of goodness from the world, I saw no reason for remaining in a world that was only interested in promoting evil and wickedness. I could no longer see any point in trying to spread any Word of goodness to a world of flesh that seemed more desperate than ever to remain under evil control.

Having witnessed the desperate evil lurking in the hearts of the hell spirits, I could now clearly see that although the world openly pretended to promote the objectives of goodness, the spirits of the world are anti-good, anti-God, and only interested in evil. Nothing could have prepared me for the extent of evil, which was now visible to my very eyes. I realised that not only is the flesh the temple of evil; the flesh is also by nature evil and unless the flesh dies the spirit can never rise to live. Through His continuous revelations, the Lord opened my eyes to see clearly that all flesh are desperately evil because the flesh is the sinful nature inherited by Man in the fall and as such only interested in proclaiming the evil works of Satan. The flesh as a nature of sin is constituted to obey the commandment of sin and as such antichrist, which explains the reason why no flesh was on my side.

Still in revelation mind of these things, I continued running to escape the evil world of flesh. However, although it seemed as if I was gaining quick pace, I discovered I had only managed to run a few metres on foot before reaching a junction that I call to this day: The Junction of the Final Frontier. As soon as I reached this junction, I discovered I was no longer able to continue running, instead I began ushering forth words of mysteries from my tongue and the battle at this point became extremely intense. The only weapon of warfare in this battle remained words and when it came to words, I always had the right word to counteract all the wicked arrows that were now coming at me from every angle of the world of flesh. I could see all the hell spirits visibly around me burning in the fire from the swords of fire coming from my tongue. I had boldness and a determination difficult to explain by any means and I felt like I had some kind of power that I myself was unable to comprehend.

As the battle further intensified, I saw thick darkness fall upon the earth and the whole world smelled as if I was in the midst of some countless decomposed dead bodies. Even though I was totally in the spirit, I was also fully naturally conscious and at the back of my mind, I kept remembering the threats of the principality-heads that they would lock me up in a mental institution if I refused to join them. I was conscious of the fact that to ordinary minds my actions and reactions were bound to be considered nothing short of madness and bearing this in mind, I tried as much as possible to act normal. However, normality to my entire being at this point was all about attacking my enemies with arrows of consuming fire and the more I tried to act normal in this sense, the more abnormal I was starting to appear. Everyone in the world of flesh was against me and the more spiritually normal I tried to act in defence of their attacks against me, the more I was beginning to appear mad to their ordinary eyes.

It wasn't long before I saw the ambulance heading my way from a distance and I knew immediately what their mission was. Soon after the ambulance arrived, the police also joined them. Since the beginning of my revelations, no one appeared human again. Everyone had strange looking faces, shapes and appearances. The heads of the police officers and that of the ambulance attendants, whose mission was to take me to the hospital, were like that of a wolf. Even though their heads in the spirit were like that of the wolf animal, I could see the unsuspecting natural human beneath the wolf darkness order. I calmly tried as naturally normal as I could to communicate to their human side to prevent them from taking me to the hospital. I desperately wanted to assure them that I was not mad by calmly giving them some natural information about myself to convince them that I am indeed extremely normal and not at all insane. However the more I tried to convince them with my natural explanations that I was not mad, the more I realised spiritually, that they were determined to take me to the hospital, no matter what I did or said.

I felt as if I was living in two worlds simultaneously. On one hand, I was fully victorious, indestructible and unstoppable. On the other hand it looked as if the principality-leaders were gaining ground and no matter what I did, it was as if they were after all going to succeed in locking me up in a mental health hospital for the rest of my stay on planet earth. Whilst I felt totally victorious in the spirit, it seemed as though there was nothing I could do to ever proclaim or enjoy this victory in the natural world. Before I knew it, I was handcuffed and forcibly put in the ambulance vehicle to be driven to the hospital.

As I was being taken to the hospital, it finally dawned on me that what I had feared most and tried all along to prevent since the beginning of my revelation was actually now happening. I was heading to a mental health hospital even though I wasn't mad. As I began to ponder on what was happening to me, I suddenly became reassured that since God did not give me a spirit of insanity there is no way anyone can certify me as mad for the rest of my life. With this reassurance repeatedly playing in my mind, I became convinced in my heart that the principality world of flesh would never succeed in certifying me as insane for the rest of my life.

I also became very certain in my mind that I would somehow come out of the mental health hospital and find my way back to heaven to rest and abide with the Lord for eternity. In my renewed hope and assurances, I felt stronger even though I was at the same time somehow weak. As the ambulance continued to head toward the hospital, I tried as much as possible to focus my mind on the beauty and the glory I had witnessed in heaven. From concentrating my mind on heaven and not what appeared to be the end of the road for me, I became more assured in my mind that there is absolutely no way the principalities forces would succeed in denying me the benefit of proclaiming and enjoying my God given victory in any dominion realms to the glory of God.

CHAPTER EIGHT
IN THE NAME OF JESUS

"And being found in fashion as a man, he humbled himself, and became obedient unto death, even the death of the cross. Wherefore God also hath highly exalted him, and given him a name which is above every name: That at the name of Jesus every knee should bow, of things in heaven, and things in earth, and things under the earth; And that every tongue should confess that Jesus Christ is Lord, to the glory of God the Father".

—Philippians 2:8-11

To further weaken me and dash my new found heavenly hope, the hell spirits continued to wage heavy war against me whilst I was being driven to the hospital.

I struggled many times to free myself physically from the handcuffs but the more I tried, the tighter they got. The journey to the hospital seemed like travelling through uncountable warfare darkness regiments and my spiritual revelation experience continued at the back of the ambulance all the way to the hospital. I discovered in my spiritual revelation journey that the universe is like a house with many doors to uncountable realms. I saw many open doors and I found myself speedily journeying in and out of the darkness regimental realms of the world. I saw the word 'Victory' in each regiment following some quick fierce attacks on me by the regiment spirits. As soon as the word 'Victory' appeared, the door of the regiment quickly disappeared, only for me to find myself in another darkness regiment full of attacking hell spirits.

As the ambulance continued to make its way to the hospital, I progressively journeyed from one spiritual regimental realm of darkness into another. In the realm of wind, it seemed as if heavy winds were going to succeed in blowing me into pieces. However, to God be the glory the word 'Victory' soon appeared and the door of the realm of wind disappeared, only for me to immediately find myself in the regimental realm of familiar spirits. Again it wasn't long before the word 'Victory' appeared and as soon as it appeared, I quickly found myself in another darkness regiment. The darkness regimental realms I journeyed in and out of seemed endless and they included the realms of magic, witchcraft, sound, fire, ocean, troubled rivers, deadly trees and many more. In the regiment of witchcraft, I saw many warlords instructing several evil spirits to generate lethal drugs and killer medicines for the sake of spreading them in the world to completely destroy human minds. I continued journeying in and out of the darkness regiments as we drove to the hospital to the extent that I was no longer able to keep track of the regiments because they seemed so many. When the ambulance finally arrived at the hospital, I found myself in what appeared to be the ultimate realm of darkness, which is the sea-realm. The first thing I noticed when I found myself in this realm was that right alongside the sea-realm, is the time-realm. Soon after the ambulance arrived at the hospital, some strange looking beings came and took me off the ambulance to a place I figured to be a waiting room.

From the moment I found myself in the spiritual realm of the sea, I became fully conscious of what was going on in the realm of time and sea simultaneously. It felt as if I was now consciously living in both worlds at the same time as a prisoner with no means of escaping from either the realm of sea or time. Unlike the previous regiments whereby the word 'Victory' quickly appeared once I found myself in the realm, it seemed for some strange reason, my password 'Victory' was never going to appear in the realms of the sea and time.

The hospital waiting area was full of wolf-headed looking beings standing everywhere, as if on guard to prevent my escape. I kept looking around, wondering how finding God could land me in a place such as this instead of a place of green pastures as I had originally thought. As I continued to look around hoping to find some escape route, my eyes caught a normal looking human being who did not appear to have the head of a wolf. I immediately tried signalling to him to help me escape from both the realms of time and sea. However as soon as I called to him for help, the Lord focused my eyes intently on him and I realised that his head was also like the wolf animal just like the rest of the beings in the waiting area. I realised none can be trusted and decided it was best to plan my escape by myself.

I progressed in my vision of revelation in the hospital's waiting area and saw that the sea-world was heavily occult and each occult regiment has a beastly World Order agenda. In segments of rotation, I saw faces of past and present world leaders as they journeyed into time from the sea to fulfil their World Order purpose and I saw them melt back into the sea once they completed their World Order purpose. I then saw a very fierce looking sea head rising from the sea into time. This World Order sea-head has a global governmental world agenda, with an ultimate aim of bringing hell fully to the surface of time, for the final reign of the beastly-order of darkness across the global world of time. I saw several faces from the occult World Order line-up to occupy their ruling positions under the beastly World Order system. They appeared desperate to serve under the beast and seemed determined to hold on to evil powers. They had a terrible mean look on their faces and seemed desperately committed to the globalisation of evil in the world.

As I continued in my revelation in the hospital waiting room, the hell spirits carried on attacking me in both realms of: sea and time. I responded audibly with the only weapon I had, which was the words of 'fire' from my tongue. However, although in reality sense I was responding in the normal way that I should, my reactions and actions continued to appear as totally out of character in the natural sense of man. I realised that if I visibly continued to respond in the same way and manner to the spiritual attacks I was facing, the evil spirits of the world that were hidden behind the human mask would indeed have an excuse to make an insanity case against me in the realm of time. With this constantly playing on my mind, I somehow came to the realisation that I did not need to say what I had to say audibly for it to have an effect on my invisible enemies.

So, after my realisation, I decided to change my action and reaction tactics to the constant attacks I was facing. I became quiet in the visible but spiritually audible in my defensive and attacking words against my spiritual opponents. From the moment I changed my tactics, I quickly recognised that my enemies hated my new spiritual strategy. Since their main aim was to make me act out of character so as to make an insanity case against me in the realm of time, they quickly increased their attacking efforts the moment I changed my strategy. However, once I had identified this to be their ploy, I stayed relatively calm in the visible and continued to respond silently with my spiritual attacking words of 'fire'.

Following my being in the waiting room for what seemed like eternity, someone with a wolf-head came and took me to a doctor whose head was also like that of the wolf animal. The first question the doctor audibly asked me in the realm of time was: "Are you hearing any voices and can you see anything"? In the sea-realm, I heard him say:

> Join us and we will let you go. If you refuse we will drug you and turn you into a killer-robot machine. You may have overcome all the other realms, but you cannot escape the sea and time-realm because the sea is the invisible dark prison of hell and time is the visible aspect of that dark prison. It is impossible for anyone existing in time to escape from the entire realm of hell, which consists of the sea and time because to be in time is to be locked firmly in the prison-realm of hell.

As he carried on with his spiritual threats, I recognised that what he wanted me to do to was audibly respond to his invisible statement which of course would make me appear as if I was speaking out of context therefore arm him with what he needed to diagnose me as someone that is hearing 'voices' and as such insane. From the moment I recognised this to be the basis for their warfare tactics, I quickly learnt to make all the necessary adjustments to prevent the evil spirits from having any excuse of labelling me insane. With extreme determination to beat them at their own game, I calmly responded to the wolf-headed doctor's silent words with silent words of attack and defence. To his audible question of whether I was seeing things or hearing voices, I answered, 'No' and I further added, "I would like to go home because there is nothing wrong with me". To make me act out of character, the spirit behind the human mask, portraying himself as a doctor pushed ahead with his game of silent words of abuse and audible normal line of questioning, but no matter how he probed, I did not give him the reaction he wanted in the visible.

Eventually, out of obvious frustration, he angrily said he needed to give me some medication to calm me down. When I refused, he sternly said, "It is either tablets or injection". I then heard him spiritually audible but visibly silent say:

You have no choice. You may think you are smart but we are smarter than you and you cannot beat the masters of the game at their own game. Our game is a simple game of mind games. The medication will help you play along better and if you reject the tablets we will inject you. Welcome to hell on earth the land of evil and wickedness. If you decide to join us, then I will free you but since you have decided to be stubborn, you will suffer immensely and you cannot escape. As I said, you have no means of escaping from the realm of sea and time. That was so smart, I mean, you trying to drive and run out of the time realm straight into heaven! No human can travel back and forth in time in the natural body, so how do you plan to escape? Time and sea are the adjoining realms of hell and unless you pass through both realms simultaneously, you cannot make your way to the heavenly realm of life. By the way, have you heard from God lately? We told you He would abandon you but you did not listen. Join us now and save yourself from unnecessary pain and suffering.

After he finished speaking both audibly and inaudibly, I responded to his silent spiritual words in the appropriate naturally silent spiritual audible manner. As for his open statements concerning giving me medication, I calmly responded by saying, "I do not want any medication, but since I am sure you are bound to inject me if I refuse the tablets I will take them". Soon afterwards, I saw someone with a wolf head walk in with the tablets meant for me, and a glass of water. As soon as I took the tablets, I realised I was no longer conscious in the time-realm and found that I was now only conscious in the spiritual sea-realm. I desperately wanted to remain conscious in both realms but upon taking the medication, I simply was unable to maintain my consciousness in the realm of time.

With my total consciousness now in the sea-realm, I continued to face heavy attacks from sea-world hell spirits who seemed uncountable in number. When I finally came back in time-consciousness, I found myself lying on a hospital bed in a mental health ward. I discovered I had started my monthly menstrual cycle while I was unconscious in the time-realm and now lying on a bed sheet actually in a pool of blood with no form of protection. It was not long after I came back into time consciousness when someone also having the head of a wolf came to change the bed sheet.

The moment I regained consciousness in the realm of time, I began seeing many robotic human looking creatures marching up and down the hospital corridors and they seemed to no longer care for anything. As I continued gazing around to familiarise myself with my environment, I saw the words 'Holy

Ghost' written on the wall of the room I was in with a marker pen. Seeing this gave me some assurance that Christ was with me and would remain with me no matter where I am. I heard a voice telling me to only take liquid and abstain from food until I leave the hospital and as a result I only had liquid throughout my stay in the hospital, which was about a total of two weeks.

From the moment I found myself in the journey of revelation, time, years and days no longer seemed to exist or have any relevance. It felt as if I had been catapulted into a new world of perpetual circles, whereby dates, time and years no longer existed. However even though it seemed as if I had no means of escaping from the circle sea-world of evil, I continued to frantically search for escape routes out of the mental health hospital. I paced up and down determined to walk out of the exit door the moment I got the slightest chance. However each time I got close to the exit door someone would immediately appear to take me back to the room that I had been admitted to. After some time, I gave up on escaping from the hospital through the exit door. I surrendered all to God and settled down in the room that they had placed me in.

Once I had decided to surrender all to God, I began spending most of my time in prayer and meditation and soon afterward started seeing myself in all kinds of 'Victory' parades. However, whilst I was on one hand seeing myself in all kinds of victory parades, on the other hand I continued facing heavy attacks from all kinds of evil spirits. Nights were the worst times and to counter the attacks of the enemy, I always stayed awake throughout the night. Right in the midst of my night battles, I would see someone physically outside my hospital room flashing a flashlight through the glass panel of my room door as if to warn me that they are watching me. In the mornings, strange looking hospital staff would routinely bring round the knockout drugs and usually try to persuade me to use them on the basis that it was for my own good. Each time they brought the medication, I would politely refuse to take it and instead of forcing me they would leave it on top of a small cupboard that was in the room as if to tempt me with it.

The evil hell-regiments continued with their tactics to try and make me act out of character so that they could have further excuses to certify me permanently insane. In their desperation they sought assistance from other cosmos dark regiments to help them put me to sleep but every one of their efforts failed. They sent several demons to scare me into reacting out of the ordinary. However instead of reacting, I simply carried on in my silent words of prayers and by being prayerful, I continued seeing myself in different kinds of victory parades. From the moment I began focusing myself on prayers and prayerful meditation unto the Lord, I discovered that my silent prayers were like a tormenting raging fire upon the evil sea-spirits and as a result I was totally convinced that their entire evil ploy was now to get me to cease fire.

As I continued in my prayers and meditation, my eyes further opened to see that the World Order of time, which happened to be the poisonous tail of the beast was far more desperate than the principality sea-heads to keep me locked up in the hospital. They made several attempts to provoke a violent reaction from me and the more I remained calm the angrier and frustrated they got. No matter their wicked attempts to distract or prevent me from concentrating on my prayers and meditation, I remained focused on praying without ceasing. The more I prayed the more the demons locked in the different bodies of the flesh, desperately pleaded with the World Order of time to let me go. As I continued in my silent prayers, I began seeing the smiling faces of many saints. Seeing their smiling faces made me feel completely liberated even though judging from my natural circumstances, it seemed like I was totally trapped with no chance of escaping from the sea-world of hell.

Having been in the hospital for what appeared to be time on end, I consciously decided to phone one or two friends to inform them that I was in hospital. I later realised that this was a mistake on my part because the moment one of them turned up to visit me, the strange looking hospital staff quickly pulled the person aside to persuade the person to convince me to take my medication. As if under hypnosis the next thing this person said after saying their hello was. "Why are you not taking your medication? Why not take them so that they can allow you to go home"? I already knew that none was on my side in the world of flesh but from a human perspective, I thought it was a good idea to inform one or two people that I was in the hospital. Following this experience, I became even more convinced that the entire ploy of the sea-realm spirits was to turn me into an addict of their crippling medication, by somehow persuading me to take it willingly rather than forcing me to.

As what seemed to be endless day and night of evil passed by, I continued to politely refuse to take any of the medication they habitually gave me and as always, they routinely left it on top of the cupboard in the room that I was in. After what seemed like infinite time in the hospital, I gradually started to get increasingly angry with God about my hospital admission. I felt so tired and weak from living on liquid for what seemed like days on end and I had also lost so much weight. I could not help wondering in my mind why God would permit me to go through what I was going through for 'goodness' sake. I felt I have had just about enough of my experience and wanted things to return back to the normal life I had before all this began. I was even angrier for the fact that no doctor had come to see me since I regained consciousness to give me an indication of when I was likely to leave the hospital. To make matters worse, there seemed to be no end in sight to the heavy spiritual attacks geared toward me by the hell spirits and the whole atmosphere continued to smell terribly as if I was living in the midst of countless decomposed dead bodies.

Blinded by my human anger, I decided to hang my praying fighting gloves and concentrate on finding an escape route out of the hospital. Since I was in both sea and time-realm simultaneously, I could see many routes in the sea-realm that appeared to lead out of the sea and also saw many routes in the time-realm that appeared to lead straight out of the hospital right back into my house. I soon discovered that the sea-realm escape routes were nothing but revolving doors, which only led to the land of nowhere and the time-realm routes, which appeared to lead straight from the hospital to my house, were all an illusion appearing as real escape routes. In my utter desperation, I decided to simply walk out through the main exit door and was adamant no one would succeed in stopping me from leaving. As I started making my way toward the main door in total blind fury, I heard the evil spirits saying, "Now she is falling for it".

The moment I heard what the evil spirits began saying, I got angrier and for the first time since I became conscious of the hospital surroundings I started praying out loud in 'tongues'. As I began praying out loud I heard the evil demons cry out, "Stop her, let her out of here, the whole place is in deep heated fire". Suddenly I saw a number of strange looking hospital staff running toward me and in my determination to escape; I decided to make a run for it. It was not long before they caught up with me. When they caught up with me they dragged me back into my hospital room, pinned me down and forcibly injected me. As I felt the injection needle go through me, I began screaming the Name of Jesus repeatedly. From the moment I repeatedly shouted out the Name of Jesus, it was as if balls of fire started tumbling down from everywhere and I could see that both the sea and time-realms were in deep heated fire.

I heard the demons lurked in the human flesh plead with the World Order to allow me go but they refused. I soon realised that the human World Order government combined with the World Order demonic celebrities were crazily more evil than their invisible sea-order masters. The human World Order not only desire for evil to rule the world forever, they also believe that evil will rule the entire universe and as representatives of rulers of evil, they were unprepared to let go of their evil hope and desire to rule the universe no matter what. They were stubbornly evil and wicked minded to the extent that even when the sea-order admitted to the human World Order that it was game over, they completely refused to listen. Even when the sea-order that deceived the human World Order to make them believe that evil would have eternal universal dominion admitted to them that they had lied to them, the human World Order was adamant to carry on with their evil works. They had a terrible crazy determination and an unquenchable thirst to hold on to evil power. The human World Order was full of desperation to receive power for the purpose of ruling the entire universe and could not be bothered whether the power was from beneath the sea or from above the sea.

In their frantic search for evil powers, the Lord opened my eyes to see how the World Order man, in the final hour of time would turn to other cosmos rulers of darkness to receive powers. They desperately searched for powers from the sea from beneath the earth and above the earth from the cosmos warlords, in the mind belief that the combination of powers from the entire sea-world would enable them to rule the universe with evil for an everlasting period. The Lord also opened my eyes to see the atrocious evil actions committed by the human World Order man at the final hours of the end-times, following their extremely wicked alliance with all the sea-realm warlords. I saw an extremely evil natured end-time World Order 'man' that has the adjoining heads of entire evil, as their ruling 'heads'. Being the entire representative heads of evil, I saw how they were filled with an unquenchable passion for wicked actions that are far beyond the comprehension of ordinary human beings of any generation.

As a token expression of their evil determination toward me, the human World Order, during my intense hospital saga, continued to stubbornly resist my leaving the hospital. They ignored their demonic counterpart's plea that they should let me go for the fact that hell fire had become unbearably hot for them since my mentioning the Name of Jesus repeatedly when they were injecting me—in their desperate attempt to silence me from praying loudly in tongues. Due to their wicked intentions to permanently render me useless in the human world, the World Order man was adamant to keep me locked up in an insane realm. Out of desperation to render me insane for the rest of my life, they sought help from one alien cosmos warlord to another, but none could overcome the power of the Lamb Jesus.

One of such cosmos spirit warlord they sought help from, came as a man and hid inside a room close by to my hospital room.

He tried to remotely toy with my mind from his hiding place. When he saw that he was not succeeding, he commanded a female patient that was a carrier of many legions of demons to enter my hospital room and taunt me into violent reaction. This is so that I would be taken into a more secure ward and be administered a stronger dosage of their medication. This woman, the legion carrier, came as was commanded by the alien warlord to fulfil her mission, but with so much 'fire' around me, she soon fled with her demons. As she fled away from me with her legion of demons, a terrible smell emanated from within her and not long afterward, I saw a man run out of a room close by to the room that I was admitted in. With my spiritual eyes open, I was able to see the cosmos-order spirit that sent the woman hiding in the human male body, and in a silent spiritual tone of voice; I asked why was he also fleeing? His spiritual answer to me was, because he does not want to end up smelling like the woman loaded with legions of demons.

In their desperate heart of evil to destroy me, the human World Order sought assistance from several other cosmos warlords. However, once they came under immense Holy Ghost fire, they would all speedily surrender and take their exit, leaving the human World Order to their evil misery, but not before acknowledging with their heads bowed that, "Jesus is Lord. Victory belongs unto the Lamb of God".

Just when it was beginning to look like there would never be an end to my ongoing battle with hell, everything suddenly subsided. The moment everything subsided, the visible atmosphere of the hospital changed. I saw many of the patients physically matching up and down past my hospital room and I could hear the spirits in them say, "We take back your fears, now have mercy for the place is too hot". I could also see many angels in huge white robes all around me. I also saw for the first time since being in the hospital the shining face of the Lord and I heard Him say:

Rejoice! It is well, for you have declared your victory in every realm. Your power of victory is in the Name of Jesus, for in the Name of Jesus all spirits in all realms and dominion must confess that I, Jesus Christ, I am Lord. You will soon leave, and henceforth, you will see that the battle was never yours but all that you have experienced is to make you a perfect witness of I AM.

The moment everything subsided, several of the hospital patients started coming to my room, asking for prayers and some even had their Bibles with them, and wanted to read it in my hospital room. Amongst the patients who came to my room for prayers was a woman who came under the pretence that she wanted me to pray for her. However, the Lord opened my eyes to see that various witchcraft spirits were in her and she only got herself admitted in the hospital to administer poison into the spirits of the already 'dead' patients, to prevent them from ever waking up from their deep sleep. As soon as she realised that her identity was no longer a secret to me, she confronted me spiritually. She stated that since my admission into the hospital ward she had constantly suffered interruptions when trying to administer her poison. She said no one seemed to be able to withstand whatsoever power is in me and that she has had to summon an emergency witches' meeting, in order to stop me from causing her any more problems.

She also said she would be going away to attend the meeting over the weekend and upon returning, she would be in a better position to 'handle' me. She then left my hospital room promising to return after her witches meeting to deal with me. Soon after she left my hospital room, I heard an angel of the Lord say, "The Lord blinded her eyes not to see your Word of victory in the witchcraft realm, for her time is up and the time has come for her to receive the rewards of her evil". When next I saw the woman, I saw a permanent mark: **Eternal Death By Fire** on her head and she wandered around in the spirit-realm wailing.

The hospital patients continued with their constant visits to my room asking for prayers and my hospital room started to resemble a spiritual consultation room within the hospital walls. It no longer felt as if I was in a mental health hospital ward and strangely enough I started to enjoy my stay. Not long after the change in the atmosphere, a woman came to my hospital room and introduced herself as a psychiatric doctor. This was my first time of seeing anyone called a doctor since my being in the hospital ward. Naturally, she appeared as a very nice person and she promised they would be discharging me as soon as they finish their observation work on me. Since she appeared so nice, I tried my utmost best to convince her there was nothing wrong with me hoping that she would speedily sign my release papers so that I could return to my normal life.

Upon listening to all that I had to say, she reassured me once again that they would soon release me and that I should have plenty of rest and should not worry. I had been feeling the urge to write since I became consciously awake in the hospital and to pass the time I asked her if I could have some pens and paper to write with. She promised to bring me pen and paper and reassured me yet again not to worry, that everything would be fine. Although she seemed nice all the while she was talking to me, I noticed the moment she started making her exit out of my hospital room that she also had the head like that of a wolf. I had seen so much that at this stage nothing surprised me anymore.

I continued in my prayer sessions with the hospital patients. As I continued in my mission of praying for the patients, I had so much rest and peace in my mind. I was once again frequently able to hear the soft and gentle voice of the Lord and I waxed stronger in regular conversations with Him. As the doctor promised, she brought me pen and paper and I began writing down whatever came to my mind. When the doctor first brought me the pen and paper I had requested for, I asked her what the date was and she told me. From that moment onward I tried keeping track of the date. To ensure I did not lose track, I noted down the dates in my daily writings. I wrote many things—mostly praise, prayers and worship. I gave most of my writings to the patients who were now regular visitors to my room. However, I kept what I had written on the 19th, 20th and 21st of August. In the following section are the things that I wrote on a daily basis between 19th and August 21st.

At the Hospital—19th of August 2004

Holy, Holy, Holy is the Name of the Lord. As it was in the beginning, so it is now and so shall it be forevermore. Your Spirit is my reward and with Your Spirit in me, insanity can never be my portion. They've injected me and tried to manipulate my mind to take medication. I do not hate them because in their ordinary mind they believe they are performing their duties. I know you have a purpose for me coming here. My trust is in You and I know you will not let me down. I know that what the eyes cannot see, it is only you that can see it. You are my judge and my righteousness O Lord. Many darkness hell spirits are gathered against me. Have mercy on me O Lord and judge those that are gathered against me in Your wrath. Let them reap the reward of their evil and consume them with Your fire without mercy. Rebuke them with Your lightening and consuming fire. Scatter them from their foundations and destroy their evil plans over my life.

The wicked persecute me because of my desire to serve, praise and worship You. They gather false witnesses against me to make a case of insanity against me. They bruised my flesh all day long and seek to destroy my soul. You are Lord God my Holy Redeemer and no one else can help me but You. My spirit O Lord is in Your care. Take charge and free my natural being for Your supernatural glory. You are the director of my spirit and the judge of all. Judge me in Your righteousness and put my accusers to shame. Glorify Yourself in me and give me a living testimony out of all this. Bring to pass Your promises in my life and open the doorway of life for me so that I can proclaim the Gospel to the ends of the world. Enable me to abide by Your Holy Commandments and keep me in line of Your righteousness. Cleanse my heart from evil and hatred and teach me how to forgive for Your Name sake. Equip me with Your gentle character and humble me with Your mercies. Help me to stand in steadfastness always. Do not leave or forsake me.

Forgive me my sins O Lord and have mercy upon my soul always.

You are my Comforter and with You by my side, my soul is rest assured that all things shall work together for my goodness and advantage. My spirit is convinced of Your divine love for me and in full assurance of Your love; I am convinced in my heart that You are only permitting my experiences to perfect my faith. You are my Rock and Shield of protection and for You are with me, ye though I walk through the valley and shadow of death I will not to perish but testify to Your conquering power. You are my light and for You are with me I shall not be afraid of darkness. You've charged Your angels to make and prepare the way for me to march across the universe and my soul operates within Your authority and power. You are my mighty warrior and with You on my side, no weapon formed or fashioned against me shall prosper. For You are with me, I am confident darkness shall pass away and my morning of glory shall last forever.

You are my Almighty Father and through Christ Jesus, You've forever abolished death for me. You saved me by Your grace and in You I have everlasting victory. Through Christ's work of remission, I acquired Your power of resurrection and in resurrection; I am no longer subject to curses or condemnation of death. I thank You Lord for affording me hope of eternal life and blessed be Your Name for giving me Christ's resurrection power. I know through Christ Jesus, I am able to do all things, for the strength of Christ always makes me strong when I am weak. I exist to praise and worship You and by worshiping and praising You, I feel strong and exceedingly joyful. You are always my great help in time of trouble and I am strengthened by Your daily comfort. You are the Pillar of my life and as You are my Pillar, evil shall never have its way in my life.

Your grace abides with me daily and even though I am lonely as flesh, my joy and peace is always full in the company of Your Holy Spirit. You feed my spirit with Your Word and each day, You quench my thirst with Your holy water. For You are with me, I am not thirsty or hungry in my spirit and though I feel weak on the outside, in You I am strong. My soul is filled with assurance of Your divine love for me and who shall discomfort me in the presence of Your comfort? You justify me when others seek to condemn me. You accept me when others reject me. You motivate and inspire me when my circumstances discourage me. You empower me when others seek to weaken me. You sweeten my soul when others seek bitterness for my heart and mind. You put my mind to rest when others seek to make me worry. You reassure me of victory when everything appears bleak and gloomy.

You sustain me with Your living hope of eternal life in the midst of my trials and You use everything the enemy intended for my breakdown—for my breakthrough. You renew my strength and empower me to march ahead when I feel I can no longer carry on. You empower me to love when the enemy tempts me to lead me to hate, You deliver me from my erroneous outcomes and justify me in Your own righteousness. You provide for all my needs exceedingly and abundantly. You fight all my battles for me and give me success and victory in all situations. You gave Your only begotten Son to die for me, in order to reconcile me to Your Holy Spirit. You love me like no other and You are always by my side. You never desert me no matter the case or circumstance and You are always faithful in Your ways toward me. You keep me safe in Your holy pavilion and You protect me with Your 'fire'. You always answer me when I call and readily counsel and guide me each day in Your infinite knowledge and wisdom. You forgive all of my sins and heal all my infirmities.

You keep me strong when I am weak by Your dominion power and authority. You sustain me in hope of eternal life through the daily demonstration of Your graceful love toward me. You are merciful to me always and great are Your deeds towards me. You are my Ancient of Days and as my Alpha and Omega, You are the source of my beginning and my hope of a perfect end. As the Almighty God, You are the only One with power above all powers and principalities and in Your presence; I am forever assured of Your eternal security and safety. You created me in the likeness of Your own image and gave me a free will of choice. You saved my spirit from the deadly choice of the first Adam through the remission work of Your only begotten Son, Christ Jesus. You redeemed my soul from the hands of the wicked. You sent Christ from heaven to earth to fulfil Your entire divine righteous Law for my soul benefit. You avoided condemnation for me by affording my spirit the benefit of Your divine willpower to enable me to choose goodness (Christ) between good and evil. You placed me in covenant relationship with Your Holy Spirit and blessed my heart with Your good conscience.

You are the Almighty Creator, yet You treat me as Your closest friend. You are the author of my destiny and in You alone I put my trust. You predestined me for goodness and enlightened my spirit with Your wisdom and knowledge to give me understanding of Your divine ways. You accounted me the benefit of Your righteous account to guarantee me eternal life success. You are the author and finisher of my faith. You are my hope of glory. You are the reason why I live. You are my holiness, my sight and my vision. You justify me on account of Your righteousness when others seek to condemn me on account of my carnal nature. You are compassionate and merciful toward me when others are merciless towards me. You make me laugh when others seek to make me weep. You are always there for me, enabling me daily to rise above all my trials and tribulations and in the midst of all that I face. You perfect Your knowledge of faith in me. You are my teacher, my righteousness and my Redeemer. You are the love of my life and the joy of my soul.

You are my, everything, O great One of the universe. I am certain of Your love and convinced of Your mercy for me in my soul. Your joy is my strength and my spirit is filled with gladness in full knowledge of Your divine love for me. In Your Holy Spirit presence I will forever remain more than a conqueror. As my Almighty Father, You made way for me where there seemed to be no way and no one can deny me my spiritual progress, for You are always with me. Your authority and power is above all powers, authority and dominion. And if You are for me, who can be against me? You are Lord God, my banner and victory and since I became convinced in my spirit that Your mighty power is causing both good and evil to work together for my good, I am no longer afraid of darkness for I know Your light is my shield. By the demonstration of Your graceful love toward me, my hope of eternal life victory is daily renewed and through daily renewed hope, my faith in You is continually strengthened.

In my mortal foolishness, I allowed foolish anger to drive and motivate my actions and as a consequence, even though I have won by Your blood and justification, it seems as if I haven't. To You Lord is all glory for giving me the understanding of Your immortal wisdom. To realise in this day that this battle is indeed for my spiritual advantage and not to my disadvantage. In this battle, You have opened my eyes to see the hidden secrets of life and why else would You do such a thing if not to convince me that I have found special grace before Your throne of grace. In conscious knowledge of Your divine graceful love for me, my soul is now rest assured that You permitted this battle to confirm my soul in eternal life justification, victory and privileges You predestined me to have on Your own righteous account, before the foundation of the world. My spirit is in this day filled with the assurance that You are in control and since You are for me and not against me, I am fully convinced that no weapon formed or fashioned against me shall prosper.

Although I have been kept here against my will on the basis that I am insane, I know I am sane, for You have not given me the spirit of insanity but of sanity, love and righteousness in Your Holy Ghost. I have a sound mind because you govern my spirit man's heart and mind in Your righteous will. Through Your righteous will, You afforded my heart the benefit of Your good conscience. You cleansed my body from sinful filth with Your atonement blood and by Your perfect finished work of remission; You saved my soul from eternal death condemnation. My body is Your temple and my soul is Your property and since I am Yours—mind, body, spirit, heart and soul—insanity shall never be my portion. To be insane is to lack the ability to appreciate the deadly consequences of one's sinful actions. In Your Holy Spirit presence, I am no longer lacking in ability to appreciate the deadly consequences of sin for I now know that the wages of sin is death and that Your gift of life for me is Your own Body, Spirit, Mind and Heart in the nature and form of Christ Jesus.

Thank You Lord for Your perfect work of atonement by which You redeemed my soul from darkness and resurrected me from death. Through Your resurrection power, You saved me from every compressing insane belief and delivered me from my erroneous conclusions that I was alive and well when I was indeed dead. As the Creator uncreated. You are life and for the fact that Your Spirit dwells in me I am now a living soul in You and if I am a living soul in You how then can I be insane? Satan! You are a liar and I have overcome you in every realm and dominion with the power of Christ being the Only Way, Truth and Life. Father Lord, I know faithful are Your ways toward me. You are divinely purposeful in Your ways and my soul is rest assured that all You permitted to take place this day in my life under the heavens is for the perfect revelation of Your kingdom purpose for my life. In Your divine knowledge and wisdom, You direct everything to produce goodness outcomes for me. You direct and change the tides of time in line with Your predestined will of righteousness and make all things work together for Your eternal glory.

You are the Almighty, the Great I AM God—all knowing and all seeing. You see beyond the depth of the sea and width of the ocean and nothing is hidden from Your eyes. You are a God of divine justice and always fulfil Your promises. Your promises unto me are of goodness and not evil, therefore evil shall never have its way in my life. You are the lover of my soul and as lover of my soul You have justified me by Your own faith and accounted me eternal life benefit from Your righteous account. You are my Father who art in heaven and as the Omnipotent, Omnificent and Omnipresent God, You are with me on earth as You are in heaven to guide and order my steps in the right path. You are my judge and in Your righteous judgement for my soul, I am no longer subject to condemnation.

Through Your remission work O Lord Jesus, You have afforded me benefit of Your 'pass marks'. Therefore my soul is fully confident that this testing period is working in my favour to perfect my living Testimony of Your divine love for me. Lord Jesus You are my righteousness and in Your righteousness, only is holiness possible. In Your righteous presence, my soul has a lively hope and in lively hope my spirit is in anticipation of having full enjoyment of a latter day glory greater than the former. My confidence is in Your eternal love for me therefore, even though it seems I have been here for time without end, I am daily strengthened by Your eternal might and everlasting power of light. I count myself privileged that You counted me worthy to reveal these things to.

The fact that You have reveal these things to me, I now know that human life on earth is an invisible battle minefield and only You can save and redeem our souls from the invisible wicked hell spirits that are on earth. Lord God You are the King of glory and as King of glory, the mighty warrior. The battle Lord God is Yours and since You are with me as the everlasting power, authority and dominion that is above all powers and authority I know I am forever a winner in Your presence. The world is against me because You love me so much. Your light is my armour and shield and if You are for me, the world's wicked will and destructive plans to destroy my soul shall never prevail. All power belongs to You, Lord God and in You I am forever more than a conqueror.

As the self-existing Creator Uncreated, You are forever above all principalities, powers and all dominion and authority is subject to Your will and power. My soul rests and abides with You in the highest place of Your secret habitation; therefore no wicked rulers of the world shall prevail over me. You are my salvation O Lord, my light and my shield. You are my foundation and my rock. You are the Ancient of Days and being the Great I AM, both good and evil is subject to Your control Lord, God. You are divine in Your wisdom and majestic in Your ways. You refine my spirit with Your refining fire and as my spiritual goldsmith; You are only permitting this fiery trial to add Your holy spiritual value to my life now and for eternity. Great is Your loving kindness and mercy toward me O my everlasting Father. You, the God of Abraham, Isaac and Jacob are my

God and with You Lord, nothing shall be impossible.

As my judge and Redeemer, I pray Lord God that you prove me always on account of Your own righteousness as Your elect in all dominion realms. Liberate me from every darkness incarceration and release my entire being from every prison cell that is beneath the sea or above the sea. Let the whole world know for a memorial record, from generation to generation till the end of days that I serve a living God. Father Lord, You are my everlasting just God. Justify me O Lord for the goodness sake of Your name. You are my defence my deliverer and You are forever my eternally perfect Holy Redeemer. Although I feel like a prisoner, I know I am free for You have liberated my soul from entire bondage. Your joy is my strength and no one can take the joy that I have in You away from me. I will hold on to You O Lord and keep praising and worshiping You. I will always glorify Your Name and always worship You before Your Throne of grace.

You are a wonderful God and in my testing period, I have come to realise that You are much more wonderful than I could ever comprehend in my mind. You have kept my spirit safe in Your secret abode and have given me refuge in Your holy pavilion. You have empowered me to walk in complete victory and have built a wall of consuming fire, defence and protection around me. When I had no strength to carry on, You enabled me in Your power to carry on in victory. When I was sad and sorrowful, you kept me fully joyful in Your Holy Spirit presence. O my Father Lord, who art in heaven, hallowed be Your Holy Name. I thank You for Your mercy and I bless You for Your loving kindness. I thank You Lord for fulfilling Your promises toward me. As divine majesty, I salute You, for You are mighty in battle and a great comforter. If not for Your comfort and power of redemption, where would my soul be?

My God You are faithful, and blessed is Your Holy Name forevermore. You promised never to leave nor forsake me and You have always been faithful to Your Word. When the whole world rejected me and was up against me, You were there to see me through the valley and shadow of death. You are my light, my truth and my way to everlasting peace. You are my joy, peace and rest. I thank You Lord for Calvary and for the remission of my sins. I thank You for keeping me in the sanity of Your loving heart. In all that I have experienced, I have come to see more of Your divine compassion and loving mercies. Therefore, unto You only will I give all glory, honour and praise now and forevermore.

Have mercy on the human souls that are walking around in this place O Lord. You know who they are and know them by their real names. You know O Lord the purpose You created them for. Only You can forgive. Only You can heal and Only You can save. All powers in heaven and earth are under Your controlling power and with You nothing shall be impossible. Have mercy O Lord and deliver the many souls in the possessive hands of the wicked spirits from the hands of their captors. Be gracious to the suffering souls and show them Your loving compassion. Set them free from the spirits that are troubling their minds. Lead them, change them, and enable them to have Your power to be able to resist the evil commands of the wicked. Help the helpless and save the troubled souls from the wicked beings.

You are the only One that can save and redeem and the only One that can deliver a soul from the dungeon of hell. No man can battle in their flesh and win against the hidden evil principalities that occupy the human mind, to permanently bury the spirit in their darkness graveyard. You are the only One that can heal the minds of the oppressively depressed. The battle of their mind is a spiritual one and unless You free their minds from the devilish oppression and depression, they are incapable of freeing themselves from their wicked mind tormentors. As the Almighty God, the Creator you are the only One that has the power of victory and unless You give these souls Your victorious power, they will remain enslaved in the darkness-world of evil. All knowledge and power belong to You and my prayer O Lord is that You enable these disabled spirits so that they, too can testify to the power of Your forgiving love. Thank You Lord for all that You have done since I got here. Thank You for revelation. Thank You Lord for perfecting my faith and hope in Your majestic divine love for me.

O Lord, Jesus Christ, Your Name is all power and You are my personal Lord and Saviour. You are always faithful and ever present. Even though I feel physically weak I am very strong in You. As my soul Redeemer, You are my Only perfect friend. My soul is fully protected from the harmful effects of the arrows of the wicked because You are with me. Your Spirit is my Comforter and with Your daily comfort I am entirely peaceful, joyful and restful in my heart, mind, body, spirit and soul. My spirit is safely secure inside Your Holy Spirit and in Your presence, I am forever confident of walking in Your everlasting victory. My faith is in You O Lord Jesus and in You only do I put my trust. I will keep holding on to You now and forevermore, for I know You will never put me to shame. The devil is a liar and because Your Truth is in me, I have overcome the entire wicked lies of the devil in all dominion and dimensional realms. You are my truth and as my truth, You are my refuge and shield.

You are always faithful in Your ways toward me and in soul conviction of your faithful ways, I am rest assured that You will surely see me through the darkness hour as my light and soul Redeemer. In Your Name every knee must bow and every tongue in heaven and on earth shall confess that You are Lord. As my Lord, You are the One with all power and in Your presence; no stronghold can ever prevail against me. Your Presence in me is the assurance of the victory I have in this world and in eternal life forever. O Lord my Saviour, how shall I praise You today? My spirit is full of gladness in Your presence and through Your perfect comfort I am exceedingly strong even though I feel weak. I worship You my Lord, in my soul and in my spirit for You are forever worthy to be praised and worshiped. Glory be to my Lord Jesus who keeps me strong and steady with His powerful Hands.

Lead me in the way ahead O Lord, and do not let me trip or fall. Afford me your successful outcomes in all that I go through and keep me in the steadfast walk of faith with You. Be Gentle with me in your chastening, O Lord and align my will daily with Your perfect will. Equip me daily with Your knowledge and wisdom and protect me always with Your Authority and power. Enable me to have perfect understanding of Your divine ways and inspire me daily to fulfil Your divine purpose for my life. Perfect my testimony of Your love through keeping me in covenant relationship with You daily and in my trials. Help me overcome the temptations of the flesh. Let Your Holy Spirit guide me daily in the path of Your righteousness and always keep me in Your holiness. Direct my thoughts daily with Your power of life and lead me in Your divine mercy to exemplify Your loving ways and kindness. Let Your goodness rule and dominate my heart always. Manifest Your glory upon me so that the whole world will see that I have found grace before You. Feed me daily with Your Word and cleanse me each day with Your Holy blood of atonement. Enlighten me with Your knowledge and wisdom and motivate me to act and react in line with Your divine will and purpose for my life.

Watch over my spirit and cure my immaturity with Your divine counsel. Perfect me with Your Word of power and let Your Word flow in me like 'rivers of life'. Lead me by Your Holy Spirit and protect me with Your full armour. Surround me with Your wall of 'fire' and enable me to praise and worship You for who You are now and forevermore. Praising You is my source of strength. Worshiping You is the reason why I live. Glorifying You is the purpose of my existence and pleasing You is all that I desire. Keep me in check and help me to accurately discern, good from evil, so that I would always make the right choices. Comfort me in

Your loving kindness and strengthen me daily with Your power. Keep me in line of faith and remove from me every spirit of fear and doubt. Convict me daily in Your loving kindness.

Take not Your Holy Spirit from me and let me always be of a sound mind. Make all that looks impossible possible and let me always dwell in Your presence. Enable and empower me to always stay focused on You. Be my everyday guide, guard and helper. Deliver me daily O Lord from evil. O Lord God my Redeemer, scatter all that gathers against me from their foundations. They gather in vain for their gathering is not unto You. You have elected me unto Yourself for the sake of Your glory therefore; You are always my defence and refuge. My soul shall praise You all the days of my life. No matter the circumstance, my tongue shall sing unto you songs of worship everlastingly for You are My Father and God. You are all I need and You are all I have. I will always hold on to Your graceful garments and will always remember Your eternal life promises unto me.

Sanctify me O Lord and keep me safe in Your Holy sanctuary. Abide with me always for Your goodness to be seen in me all the days of my life now and forevermore. Crown me with glorious success and robe me with Your garment of praise forever. My soul testifies to Your presence in me and since You are in me, who shall I be afraid of? The Lord is the lover of my soul and as lover of my soul He will not allow any evil to befall me. My spirit is in vision of Your multitude of warring angels that are around me and my spiritual eyes can see Your protective wall of 'fire' surrounding me. Who can prevail against Your warring angels or penetrate through Your consuming wall of fire to harm me? You have nullified the power of the wicked and have given me Your victorious authority to prevail in my trials against the evil and the wicked. Therefore, no weapon of evil fashioned against me shall prosper for in the Lord, I am forevermore more than a conqueror.

Unto You Lord, do I commit all that pertains to my existence, for You are my Creator, Merciful King and Father who is forever the greatest on deeds. You are my life and as my life, the lover of my soul. With You by my side, my soul is everlastingly in abundance of life. Make a way for me, Lord God where there seems to be no way and let Your will of life shine forth through me, for the world to see that am forever a living soul in Your Holy Spirit. Your Spirit is upon me Lord God and in the presence of Your Spirit, my spirit is full of Your glorious light. For the sake of Your goodness manifestations upon my life, end the days of darkness Lord God and magnify me fully in Your shining light of glory for the whole earth to see and testify in all generations of mankind that I am Your elect now and forevermore. Release me Lord God from this place and shine me as Your light and witness across the world.

Turn my entire test into a perfect testimony of Your loving kindness and make way for me with Your power for me to give the testimony of Your merciful grace unto to all nations. I thank You Father for Your perfect divine nature. And thank You for Your perfect will for my life. Receive my thanks and praises today with gladness and joy in Your heart. Forgive me Lord God for my foolish, fleshy wrath and give me all the understanding that I need to stay faithfully strong in all of my trials. You are my Redeemer and as my Redeemer my soul is perfectly convinced that everlasting life is my potion for You are in me, and I am in You. I thank You Lord for Your grace upon my life. I pray Lord that You forgive the nations of the world for all have sinned greatly against You. Have compassion on all the struggling minds and sorrowful faces that I see O Lord and deliver them in Your compassionate love just as You have delivered me. Set them free from their shackles and deliver their minds from their mind captors.

Have mercy Lord God on the many souls around the world and manifest Your glorious knowledge to the entire world. Lord Jesus, open the eyes of the spiritually blind to see that You are the Way, Truth and Life. Heal the spiritually crippled and enable them to walk from their darkness to You as light. Take over their minds Lord and renew their minds with Your divine knowledge and righteous power. Rain down Your fire judgement upon the wicked fallen angels and firmly imprison them in their evil and darkness cells. Now is my soul fully joyful and peaceful for I hear the sound of victory trumpets and I rejoice in the knowledge of my Redeemer's Second Coming.

I thank You Lord for Your goodness and I thank You for Your power. I thank You for Your love for me. I thank You for the air that I breathe. I thank You for the saintly stars of heaven. I thank You for the moon and the sun. I thank You for the beautiful plants and flowers. I thank You for the birds of the air and thank You for all creatures, great and small. I thank You for the beauty of heaven and for Your everlasting glory upon my life. I thank You for keeping my soul safe. Thank You for being the watchful keeper of my soul. I am grateful to You and I owe You my life. Therefore all my thanks shall be unto You now and forevermore. How shall I thank the One who saved my soul from death? How shall I thank the One who delivered and redeemed my soul from evil? How shall I thank the One who is ever forgiving and gracious unto me? Even if I had a thousand tongues, they would not be sufficient to thank You.

I love You Lord with all my heart and shall forever be grateful to You for loving me over and above my soul's expectations. Lord Christ Jesus, I thank You for healing all my infirmities and I thank You forgiving all of my iniquities. By Your perfect remission work I am fully atoned now and forevermore. Blessed be Your name, Lord Jesus now and forevermore. You are my joy and You make Your joy full in me. You are my power and You make Your power full in me. You are Merciful and Your mercy and grace follow me everywhere I go and shall continue to rest and abide with me for You are always with me. You are my righteousness and You are the reason for my strength, power and joy. You are the reason for my soul's existence and You are the author and fulfiller of my entire life destiny. With Your power of love and life I have overcome death and with Your righteous power I have overcome sin. O death where is your power? O sin where is your will? Lord Jesus, You cancelled the power of death and changed my evil nature to Your divine nature and replaced my evil character with Your perfect divine character.

Through Your perfect sacrifice, You redeemed me from death and for You have perfectly liberated my soul from the entire covenant of darkness; death has no legitimate right to oppress or rule over me for You have fully paid off the price for my sins with Your own death on the Cross of Calvary. With Your perfect sacrifice, You fulfil the law of righteousness for me and by Your fulfilment, sin no longer has legitimate power to govern my will and heart or deny my soul from enjoying the benefits of Your eternal life existence. Lord Jesus, great is Your Holy Name now and forevermore. No other name but Yours has all power thus at the mentioning of Your Name, every knee bows and every tongue in heaven and on earth will always confess that You are Lord and as Lord the everlasting God who is the same yesterday, today and forever.

Praise the Lord O my soul. Let all that have the breath of life lift up His Holy Name. Let all that have breath praise the Almighty God, Creator of heaven and earth, gracious deliverer of our souls and perfect Redeemer of life. Praise be to the King of kings who is forever ruler of my heart and soul. Praise be to my Holy Counsellor and great Comforter. Praise be to my God who is WORD and as WORD the only One with all power and authority over and above all. Praise be to the self-existing Creator Uncreated Father of my spirit. Praise be to the Most High God, Creator of the universe. I thank You Father Lord for lifting up my spirit and soul in this day and forevermore. Thank You for giving me the benefit of the fullness of Your joy. Great are Your mercies and faithfulness toward me Lord God. Amazing is Your grace and powerful is Your direct Word of counsel to my soul. Glorious are Your deeds, perfect is Your will for my life and just and equitable are Your ways. Righteousness is Your order and holiness is Your Name.

I thank You now and forevermore for who You are and always shall be to me. You are my helper and my victory. You are my Alpha and Omega and in You, I have a perfect beginning and the guarantee of a perfect end. You are my Shepherd and as my Shepherd, my provider. Therefore I shall never be in want or lack in anything that is of Your goodness. You are my All in all and You are the same Jesus Christ yesterday, today and forever. You are my light and as my light, my everlasting Lord of victory. You are my peace and in You the enemy can never succeed in their wicked efforts to sadden my spirit. You declare the end from the beginning and the outcome of Your promises to me now and forever is Your goodness for my soul in eternity.

Glory, glory and glory to the everlasting King of kings. Glory be unto God the Father who is forever the miracle worker. Glory and honour be unto my Saviour who in His perfect loving grace quickened my spirit from death back to life with His power of resurrection. Glory to God who daily renews my living hope of eternal life of peace, rest and joy. Glory be to my Redeemer who lives forevermore.

At the hospital, the 20th of August 2004

Lord Jesus, today my soul rises to thank You and declare my love for You. I love You with all my heart, soul, mind, body and my spirit. I praise You for You are worthy to be praised. You are my personal Lord and Saviour. You are my deliverer, my Redeemer and in You, I have all goodness of life. There is none like You and never shall there be any other like You. To demonstrate Your perfect love for me You died on the Cross of Calvary to release me from the claws of death. Through Your death on the Cross You fully paid all my sinful debt and released me from the wages of sin. You came from heaven to earth to overcome the world for me and in You I have also overcome the world. Through Your perfect obedience to the Father, You afforded me benefit of the Holy Spirit of the Father. And in the presence of the Father my soul is always in perfect rest. Your Name is above all names and all power is in You. With You, I am far above all principalities and powers and at the mentioning of Your Name every knees shall bow and every tongue in heaven and on earth shall confess that You are indeed Lord of my heart and soul.

Be thou glorified O Lord with my praise and worship now and forevermore. I bless You O Lord, for blessed is Your Name forever. I rejoice in the presence of Your Holy Spirit and adore Your glorious beauty today O Lord. Your glory is everlasting and it is my shining bright armour. I give You praise and honour for all power, glory and honour is Yours forever. I am Your worshiper and You are my God. I am Your clay, and You are my Potter. You are my Creator and Maker. Today my heart is full of appreciations and thanksgiving for now that I am in knowledge of Your goodness love, I am rest assured that You will always work all things out for my good. I thank You for the blood of remission. Thank You for the power of resurrection. Thank You for Your love and compassion. Thank You for Your forgiveness of my sins. Thank You for the redemption of my soul. Thank You for being the joy of my life. Thank You for Your Holy Spirit love. Thank You for the water that I drink. Thank You for Your awesome presence in my life. Thank You for every creature, great and small. Thank You, O Ancient of Days and my Lilly of the Valley. Thank You, my Morning Star, director and producer. Thank You for the beautiful flowers that You give my spirit daily from Your garden of love. Thank You for revealing to me the beauty of Your glory. Thank You Lord of lords, King of kings and God of gods.

How shall I praise You today? What can I say to exalt Your Holy Name? Your Name is above all names and Your ways towards me are excellent and perfect. O my excellent Father I am in awe of Your beauty. From having knowledge of Your love for me, I have daily strength and confidence in Your merciful grace. I feel Your presence around me daily and am peaceful in Your graceful arms. Lord God You are my mighty warrior and as my mighty warrior the everlasting victorious King of the universe. Is there a mountain higher than Your Holy Mountain? Is there a river that You cannot part? Is there a valley that You cannot make me overcome? Is there a sea too deep for my God to part or is there a place in the universe that is not within Your control? Is there a problem that my God cannot solve? Is there anything under or above the sun that my God cannot see? Is every secret of time not in Your hands? Is there anything that You cannot do? If You are with me, who can be against me? Can any river overflow me when You are with me? Can any fire burn me when You are with me?

The universe is Your house built with Your own power for Your glory and honour. As the universe is Your house built with Your own power and dominion authority, You are the only One that has the key to every door. Only You can open a door that no one can shut and only You can shut a door and no one can open it. You see all and know all. You declare the end from the beginning because You are the Alpha and Omega. Lord God for You are on my side, whom shall I fear or be afraid of? I am convinced I am triumphant in my tribulations and entirely victorious in my trials because You are always with me. O Lord my king, how mighty is Your name. You are all able, all wonder, and all glorious God of the universe. You are Amazing Grace, divine honour and powerful glory. You are the Holiness of my spirit and the righteousness of my soul. Your righteousness is the light of my soul. You are my King and Judge. You are just in Your ways and abundant in Your mercies. Your Spirit is Holy and Your goodness endures forever. You are the Great I AM and as the, I AM King, the hope of strength for the weak. You are my light and shield, my Rock and my High Tower. Your shining glory is upon me. Your peace and rest is in my soul, therefore my soul is full of Your joyful peace and rest.

You are JEHOVAH and you never leave nor forsake your elect.

You are JEHOVAH NISSI, my banner and my victory.

You are JEHOVAH ROHI, my guide and my Good Shepherd.

You are JEHOVAH JIREH, my provider.

You are JEHOVAH SHALOM, my peace.

You are JEHOVAH RAPHA, my healer.

You are JEHOVAH TISIDKEMU, my righteousness.

You are JEHOVAH M'KADDESH, my sanctifier.

You are JEHOVAH ADONAI, the self-existing God Uncreated Creator. You are the Master of the universe— defender of the faith, and defender of the faithful.

You are ELOHIM, the Creator of Heaven and Earth.

You are EL-ELYON, the Most High God.

You are JEHOVAH SHAMMAH, the One that never leaves nor forsakes.

You are the Almighty God of the universe.

In Your presence, I have everlasting victory.

You are my Refuge, my Fortress, Redeemer and Hope.

You are my joy, my power and my shield.

You are Omnipotent, Omnipresent, Omnificent and Omniscient God.

The arrows of the enemy are of no effect, for I have Your Word of power and I operate in Your dominion Word of authority. Your Name O Lord Jesus is above all names, and in Your Name my enemies are nothing but dust, which you have given me power to trample over. You are benevolent and always good on deeds. O Lord Jesus, Thank You for giving me Your victorious power. At the mentioning of Your Name, my enemies have no choice but to bow and confess that, "Greater is He that is in me than he that is in the world".

As the light of the universe, You made me a shining light which darkness cannot comprehend. Who, O Lord can come near me to harm me underneath Your graceful banner? Your Holy Spirit is the armour and shield of protection over my life. With Your fire 'power' you made me fire and as fire in You, no evil spirit can quench me or come near to harm me. You are Lord my Holy Rock of Ages and with You as my rock of protection whatsoever tries to come against me will scatter into pieces. I am like a river overflowing with abundant blessings in Your Holy Spirit and no one shall ever succeed in drying me up. Lord God, You are my banner and victory and in Your victorious presence no evil weapon formed or fashioned against me shall prosper. In Your Holy Spirit presence, I remain forever standing in Your victorious outcomes for my entire life and with You by my side; the enemy will never succeed to make me trip or fall.

O Lord God, I am nothing without Your Holy Spirit. Your Holy Spirit is the source of my life and as the source of my life my only hope of eternal life of peace, rest and joy. Lord God, take not your Holy Spirit away from me for Your Holy Spirit is the entire blessing that I have in my soul, the joy in my heart, the peace in my mind, the rest in my spirit and the power of life in my body. Your Holy Spirit is my Teacher and director of my mind. My mind Lord God is led by Your Holy Spirit mind therefore insanity has no place in my mind. My body is Your everlasting temple and as Your temple, blessed am I forever in all realms and dominion. No curse shall have power over my soul for in Your righteous account, I am free from all bondage and evil covenants. Lord Jesus, Thank You for giving me Your body, heart, mind and also Your Spirit. You are my Christ yesterday, today and forever and in You, I am forever free from every past, present and future curses.

Shine O Lord Your glorious face upon me always and have mercy upon my soul. Forgive us our sins and deliver us from evil. Lead us not into temptation and help us to overcome the entire wiles of the devil. Strengthen us with Your joy and perfect us in our afflictions. Guide us in Your Holiness and teach us Your ways. Open our eyes daily to see the way to Your heart. Help us discern right from wrong and guide us to make only the right choices. Shield us with Your power and let not the wicked one steal our joy. Strengthen our spirit daily with Your anointing power and empower us to remain faithful to You always. Keep our hope of eternal life alive and focus our eyes on Your perfect spiritual outcomes for us.

Thank You for Your loving kindness and affection towards me. Who do I have beside You and what can I do without Your Holy Spirit? You have gladdened my soul with Your joyfulness and my soul is full of joy in Your Holy Spirit presence. I am daily strong and continually strengthened by the knowledge of Your abundant love for me. I am certain I will soon leave this place as Your witness and go forth to proclaim Your Gospel across the world. I see the light of Your Morning Star shining on me, guiding me through the tunnel to come out on the other side full of Your power and everlasting glory. Therefore, I know my hope of eternal life glory is not in vain. My soul resides in Your everlasting Kingdom and in Your presence, I am triumphant over death everlastingly. All that I am belongs to You, my Lord for I am Yours, You are The One that has control over my entire life existence.

You direct everything in the realm of time from Your eternal existence and in Your loving kindness. You work out all things in all realms for my good. You are Lord God, the Master that holds the key to every door in every realm and with Your master key, You have opened Your eternal door of life for me. Therefore death shall never prevail over my soul for with Your blood You have redeemed my soul from death to enjoy abundant life in Your presence, forever. My spirit is daily reassured of Your mercies for me and in knowledge of Your merciful grace for my life, I am certain the troubles of this moment shall pass away and Your goodness and mercies upon me shall forever endure.

I praise, worship and glorify You O Lord in my trials and afflictions, for I am certain it is all working for my eternal goodness. I thank You Lord Jesus for resurrecting my soul from death. To resurrect my soul from death, You suffered for me. You knew no sin, yet died as sin to free me from the consequences of sin, which is eternal death. You are my advocate and mediator and with You, I know I will always be a winner. The enemy will only work to the promotional value of my spirit, for You have promised never to allow me depreciate but to increase me in Your blessings forever. Since You have blessed and not cursed me, I am therefore blessed wherever I am and will remain blessed no matter my earthly circumstance or situation.

Praise the Lord O my soul and I give glory to the Lord for I have found grace and favour in His presence. Who shall stand in the way of Your elect? Your calling upon my life is a 'calling' for me to have life in abundance in Your presence. Therefore, death shall never succeed in separating me from Your abundant life presence. In You Lord God, I am forever more than a conqueror. You are my Mighty Warrior and this battle Lord, is Yours and not mine. As my Mighty Warrior, You have already won the battle for me before the foundation of the world and Your victory shall remain my everlasting portion. Glory and honour be unto my Lord who is forever Mighty in battle. Glory be to the Almighty God who is everlastingly good on deeds. Lord God, my Mighty Warrior, open the gates and usher forth Your elect to march forward and deliver Your message of hope to all the nations. Bless the Lord O my soul. Blessed be His Holy Name forever. Blessed You are Lord, yesterday—now and forever. Holy, Holy, Holy is Your Name forever and evermore.

At the Hospital 21st of August 2004

Thank You, O Lord for yet another amazing day and thank You for keeping my mind, body, spirit and soul safe in Your Holy Spirit presence. Yea though I walk through the valley and the shadow of death, I will hear or fear no evil, for Your rod and staff comfort and direct me and I will remain in Your everlasting goodness path. O Lord Jesus, when You march me forward from this hellish place— keep in Your remembrance the troubled souls that I have met here. Continue to have mercy on them and where sin abounds let Your grace much more abound. By Your special grace, free them from their strong oppressors and help them to see their way out of the dungeon. Direct them in Your mind of purpose and empower them to resist the evil enemy mind-killer.

Lord God, You are love and as love the One with power and authority over all matters of life and death. My enemies are afraid, very afraid for they know I have Your grace and they have Your wrath. Fire is raging in hell and they are in deep, painful sorrow. Who shall help and save them from Your wrath for only You can save and only You can redeem. They gather O Lord against me for evil's sake, but they gather in vain for your portion for me is goodness. Therefore, Your judgement 'fire' consumes them immensely for their evil gathering. They have no Saviour or Redeemer and as such they will burn and perish in Your consuming fire everlastingly. You are my Redeemer—Lord God and whoso-ever is against me shall suffer immensely in Your judgement wrath.

Who shall stand against Your elect and not face Your wrath? For as Your elect I am the apple of Your eye. Great are Your deeds toward me and mighty is Your power of love for me. In this day O Lord, I bear testimony to Your power of salvation and deliverance. You have saved me by Your grace.

My soul is full of gladness and I rejoice for I know the Lord is for me, hence no one can be against me. Father Lord I lift up my voice today to praise and worship You. Worship and praise is Your food and my heart is full of joy, because You have given me the 'garment' of praise to always offer You perfect sacrifices of worship and praise. My mind is no longer troubled for I know You are on my side. I glorify Your Name today O Lord, for You are my Defence and everlasting God and Father. The reason I live is You. I was born in imperfection, however by grace You made it possible for me to be 'born again' and You perfected my soul and spirit in Your perfection.

You are the gatekeeper of my soul, the master-key holder of the door to my heart. The key to close and open any door is in Your Word of authority. In the Name of Jesus, the Lord has given me His authority Word of power and no door can shut on me or refuse to open for me. I see the door and the way out and I know the gate of time will be opened wide, for me to walk through and preach the Gospel across the world at the Lord's appointed time. No one can keep the Lord's elect locked up, for I am already free and liberated in my soul and spirit. My soul is in the presence of the Master of all dominion and in His dominion power and authority; my spirit shall march ahead to the glory of His Name.

I am Christ's soldier and in the Name of Jesus, I am more than a conqueror. You are my hope O Lord, my banner and victory. I adore Your Holiness and marvel at Your righteousness. You are worthy of perfect praise and worship. I exalt and reverence You today from the depth of my soul. My soul is full of joy and my songs are of victory. My battle is over and my victory parade is everlasting. Glory be to the Father, Son and Holy Spirit who is forever all glory, honour and power without end.

The symbol of my victory, Lord, is Your Holy Spirit in me. In Your Holy Spirit presence, I will praise and worship Your Holy Name forever. From Your righteous account You justified me and in Your perfect justifications, You poured Your holiness into me. Your holiness in me is evidence of Your perfect love and in soul conviction of Your love for me, my soul is triumphantly jubilant. In the brightness of Your glory upon my soul, darkness cannot stand against me. Your Holy Spirit is my light, my covering and shield. Therefore darkness can never prevail over me in the presence of Your Holy Spirit light. O Great I AM, glory be to Your power and power be to Your glory now and forever. In Your Holy Spirit is life and only in Your Holy Spirit of life are we shining lights.

Your joy is my strength and I derive great comfort and joy from praising and worshiping You. With my praise unto You, I shut the door on sadness and in worshiping You, I feel joyfully strong. My soul is lifted up when I praise You and my spirit is edified when I reverence You. I exist to praise and worship You and my soul is exceedingly gladdened through praising and worshiping You. My soul desires to exceedingly praise You today my Lord and my spirit longs to worship You for You are worthy of all the praise and worship. Accept my worship today and forevermore as a perfect sacrifice and in return increase Your powerful strength in me Lord God.

My period of affliction seems long and the days of suffering appear to be many, but when I remember Your good purposes for me, I glory in my tribulations and am exceedingly joyful for my suffering as flesh. I know my flesh must suffer to allow my spirit to walk in perfect knowledge of Your divine and faithful love for me. I know all of this is an experience to prepare me for my life's mission, which You have already made possible for me, ahead of my time. In knowledge of Your love for me, I am daily reassured of success in my mission. Moreover, in my perfect soul conviction of Your love for me, I am certain You are only permitting my tribulations and trials to enable me see clearly in all realms that nothing shall be impossible with You. I know Your love is real and I trust You will bring all of Your promises to pass because You love me.

Your love is divine and perfectly truthful and my faith is growing stronger and stronger daily in Your faithful love. My soul conviction of Your faithful love for me increases daily. My eyes continue to be opened day by day to see that all things are perfectly working together for my good. Every attempt by the deceiver to convince me that You hate me has failed, because I have remained continually convinced in my soul that You love me, hence my flesh cannot confuse my spiritual mind to believe that You hate me. In the presence of Your power of love and authority of life, I shall not lament, for Your power is the mighty strength and joy in me. I know this dark hour will soon pass and the whole world will see the everlasting shining light of Your glory upon me.

Thank You Lord for forgiving me of my sins. Thank You for saving me from the hands of the wicked foul spirits. Though my flesh tried to lead me into anger toward You because of my trials, my spirit knows You are a just God. In my ignorance I was angry with You for I could not understand that this was all because You love me so much. You destroyed the yoke of flesh anger in me with Your loving compassion and immeasurable comfort. Flesh anger only leads to self-destruction. My spirit now knows that evidence of perfect application and demonstration of Your knowledge is to allow You to take vengeance for me, for vengeance is Yours and Yours only. Love creates for goodness sakes and as God who is love, only You knows how to appropriately reward the wicked and only You knows how to fight the cause of the righteous.

Thank You Lord for affording me grace from Your loving heart and thank You for also for opening my eyes to see in the midst of my trials and tribulations, just how divinely perfect Your love is for me. Thank You for Your Holy Spirit love for me and thank You for not hiding Your perfect knowledge and wisdom from me. In focusing my mind on Your Holy Spirit love, my spirit is fully aware that wisdom of life is to totally submit and surrender all to Your perfect will of life. You are my everlasting love and as the only lover of my soul, Your will for me is eternally perfect. In Your perfect will, I am guaranteed to have a perfect goodness outcome. Therefore, every circumstance whether it is seemingly good or evil shall work together for my perfect eternal life-goodness outcome.

I submit and surrender all to You, Lord Jesus. Let Your perfect will be done for the glory of the Father, the Son and the Holy Ghost. I trust in Your will for me, for I know You are a just God and You are a God of purpose. I now know that what seems like injustice is all for a just purpose. I am a sinner and I suffer as a sinner in the flesh of sin but in Your spiritual justification for my soul, I am full of comfort. O Lord Jesus, You knew no sin yet You suffered for my sake to justify my spirit now and forever. If You, who knew no sin gladly suffered for my sins so that I would be saved, is it not proper that I who was conceived in sin, but justified by Your grace, gladly suffer as flesh for Your sake? I glory in my tribulation and worship You in my trials for I know that because I have found grace in Your presence, it is all working together for my good. By grace You called me, for Your glorious purpose of spreading the Good News of salvation to the whole world and by grace You chose me even before You 'called' me. Your hands of glory are upon me forever and my soul is full of everlasting joy in Your presence. Therefore, no principalities, powers and rulers of darkness of any kind or any wicked mind in any place can prevent Your everlasting glory that is upon me from shining forth. Your light is upon me and Your goodness is in me, so victory is mine forever and in that victory I will march forward.

In Your Name Lord Jesus, every stronghold of time and barriers of the world of darkness must come down and disappear from my way and I shall march forward to fulfil my life purpose to the glory and honour of You, my

Almighty God. Open, O ye doors, for the MIGHTY LORD OF RIGHTEOUSNESS is in me, and when the Mighty God in me commands a door to open, the door must open. For only He can open a door and no one would be able to shut it and only He can shut a door and no one would be able to open it. The WORD of God is power and dominion over all and by His power and authority, I command every gate of hell to disappear from my way. For as the Lord's temple it is written: "No gates of hell shall prevail against me". So it is written, and so shall it come to pass as it is written. Amen.

Spending my time writing, praising, worshiping and praying for the patients made me feel like I was in heaven on earth. As I continued to praise and worship, the evil spirits continued in their efforts to distract me by bruising my physical body with scratch marks. Although I could see several physical scratch marks all over my body I was no longer interested in focusing on their futile efforts because I was certain in my spirit that their scratch marks were of no harmful effect to my spiritual being. I was full of the Lord's comfort and in His perfect comfort, full of great cheer. The more I focused my mind on serving what seemingly turned out to be the Lord's purpose for allowing my hospital admission, the more strange things were happening in the area of the ward that I was admitted in. Several patients continually marched up and down outside the room I was admitted in. Some stopped by occasionally to ask for prayers and others simply marched up and down. Some of the ward staff also came to my room asking for prayers. Praying for everyone that stopped by gave me a sense of purpose and in my sense of purpose, I was totally peaceful. Everyone suddenly became very nice to me and in a strange way, I began enjoying my hospital stay much more than I could have ever envisaged.

I derived so much joy from praying for those that came seeking for prayers and when left by myself, I would spend the time gladly worshiping, praising or writing. As I concentrated my mind on serving what I had come to accept as my purpose for being in the hospital, I saw the angels around me continually increase in number and from seeing the increase; my heart became even more peacefully joyful. After a number of days the Lord said it was time to go and that I would soon be out of the hospital as the purpose of my coming there had been served.

After the Lord told me that I would soon be leaving the hospital, everyone suddenly stopped being nice to me. The attacks from the evil spirits were intensified and the World Order faces started appearing again. They were much meaner looking and seemed very determined than ever before to destroy me. To fulfil their plan they launched a terrible attack against me. However, none of their weapons had any real effect on my spirit being. The spirits hibernating in the patients and staff that I had been praying for were all in on the attack. As I battled, I suddenly found myself spiritually journeying deeper and deeper into the realm of spiritual realm of sea and time.

To my surprise, I began seeing several faces of those I had once believed to be saints now appearing as agents of the devil. I saw many spirits walking round and round the circle of time trying to find their way out of the time-realm. However, because they were also simultaneously in the sea-realm, they simply journeyed from time back into the sea and from sea back and forth throughout the realms of darkness. I saw many desperate faces seeking for power, but because they were seeking in the wrong places, they tripped and fell deeper into the darkness sea-realm.

From deeply travelling through the spiritual realms of sea and time, I was able to eventually see the entire time and darkness sea realms. Time and sea are realms of imprisonment. A spirit can only become free from this imprisonment realm if they find the only way that leads out of the prison-yard—Jesus the Christ. I realised that the main problem faced by the human spirits in the time is that once a spirit enters the realm of time, that spirit immediately becomes consciously disconnected from their imprisoned aspect that was still in the darkness sea-realm. I discovered that time itself does not change. Instead, it simply goes round and round in circles. The clock in the spiritual realm of time is stationary at the dark hour of midnight. The only way to change from the midnight dark hour to daylight time of eternity is through the freedom walk from darkness to light.

The sea dungeon has an adjoining door with other extra-terrestrial cosmos-darkness realms. The extra-terrestrials spirits have the image of the beast, for they are also part of the spiritual sea-world of darkness. In the final hour of darkness the entire terrestrial and beastly-order from the spiritual sea-world of darkness will come together and become one with humans. This is in order to render the World Order humans totally wicked with a complete evil nature and image of the entire darkness beastly creature. These terrestrial cosmos alien heads will be instrumental in bringing total darkness regimes to the earth and their activities with the World Order humans will gradually increase in the final hour of the realm of time. All spirits of the sea and of the dark cosmos realm are sad and ugly looking creatures. In their ugly and sad looking appearances, they journey in and out of the time-realm trying to find their way out of the prison of time.

The realm of time as a prison-realm of darkness is a spiritual jungle that is full of lost souls. Once a human being enters the time-prison-realm of time, they immediately become unconscious of their sea-world connections. In their unconscious state, they have no recollections of the purpose of their journey to earth. In total loss of memory and lack of understanding of who they are or where they are, human beings in the prison-realm of time, end up spending their time desperately chasing after nothing instead of choosing and following the only Way that leads from darkness to light. Due to not having any understanding of the purpose of their earthly journey from sea to time-realm, the concentration of most humans in the world is on their earthly survival. By concentrating on their earthly survival, they end up not making any spiritual progress.

The human spirits in the world that are without God's Holy Spirit are dead spirits and as dead spirits—slaves of darkness rulers. The darkness rulers control the souls of the dead spirits on the earth and deceive them to believe they are making real progress. The dead spirits believing that they are alive only see death from a natural mind perspective. They focus on building a worldly empire and those who consider themselves to have succeeded in building their world empire see themselves as powerfully strong. They spend their prison time on earth focusing on building their castles in the air only to find themselves back in their dead state in their sea-realm prison cell once they take their exit from the natural world. The only place a spirit can make the transition from darkness to light is in the prison-realm of time and a spirit will only be set free from their sea prison cell once they make the transition. The moment the dead spirit of the world melts back into the sea-realm and becomes conscious of their rotten prison cell, they immediately want to journey back into time to find their way out of darkness before the end of the 'Dispensation of Grace'.

The way out of the darkness prison is Jesus Christ and being the Way, the Truth and the Life, the antichrist world hates Him with a passion. The visible natural world of Man is a world of lies and the primary aim of the darkness rulers that are occupying the highest places of the world is to dominate man and oppress the soul of man from within. To achieve their evil aims, they are strongly against any dead spirit finding and surrendering themselves to the Truth of Christ. Therefore although the spirit of man is actually seeking for the Way, the antichrist spirit inside his soul occupies his heart with worldly desires leading his mind to strongly object to the only Truth, which is Christ Jesus. Dead spirits are spiritually insane and as insane spirits, incapable of appreciating the consequences of their actions. Due to their insane hearts and minds, they readily embrace the harmful ways of death and angrily reject the perfect way of life they journeyed to the earth to find in the first place.

The password for entering the realm of darkness is: sin. In the fall of man, Adam the forefather of man became the forefather of sin. Every person was conceived in the line of the dead Adam and as a result, spiritually dead. The password for entering the realm of light is righteousness hence Christ had to die as sin to enter into the realm of darkness to bind death for us. Through His binding of death, Christ as the Resurrection paved the way for us to resurrect from death back to life and whosoever is in Christ is no longer subject to the controlling forces of dead sprits and wicked rulers of darkness. God the Father gave us Christ, His righteousness to be our way out of darkness. Christ as God's righteousness is the fulfiller of the law of righteousness.

Therefore, He is the only means by which any spirit can resurrect from death back to life. A dead spirit cannot inherit the Kingdom of God. God as the Creator of all is a LIVING SPIRIT and as a LIVING SPIRIT only the living are heirs of His perfect Image. The dead spirits of the world although are in prison of time, see themselves as free and because they consider themselves to be free they see no need to seek freedom. God as our Creator is 'Love' and as Love, He gave us Christ to be our Ark of Salvation. Christ is God's grace and love revealed. God has to release us from death by His grace, because in death no spirit is capable of redeeming their soul and thereby resurrect from death. To reject Christ is to reject God's love and grace and whosoever rejects God's love and grace, will continue to dwell in His wrath.

As my mind continued to dwell in the understanding of these things, I carried on seeing uncountable sorrowful human looking faces, journeying to and from time and sea. The moment they enter into the time-era, they would become unconscious of their imprisonment in the sea and once they melted back into the sea, they become conscious of their sad and terribly sorrowful spiritual existence. I saw many that were being buried in the world, invisibly standing and weeping at their funerals due to their realisation that they had failed to find their way out of the realms of sea and time. In the prison-realm of time, everyone looks humanly the same on the outside, but in the dark realm of the entire sea-world, everyone looks different. Those locked in the realm of time, are in a world darkness market, trading their souls for nothing with the darkness sea-world. They go from sea to time and time to sea, all in mind of evil and wicked trading.

The method of communication between time and sea is mostly dreams but these dreams are juggled facts and information, so that the spirit that is in the time-realm would have no understanding of the dreams. Those in time are blind and cannot see anything for what it is, but those in the sea can clearly see those in time. Those in the sea are wicked toward those that are in time, and all they do is deceive and confuse them so that they would not find their way out of the sea. Whoever finds the way out of the sea-realm while still in time becomes a target of the spirits of darkness. The evil souls of the world will immediately focus on the resurrected spirits and fiercely try them with all kinds of trails to confuse and ultimately deceive them into believing God hates them so as to frustrate them into abandoning the right ways of God and return back into the wicked ways of the world.

The door from sea to time is like a very busy airport, with multitudes of souls travelling in and out daily. Deep inside the sea and time-realms, I saw many doors that simply lead from one world door of darkness to another and then back to the sea dungeon. In the time-realm I saw many going from one door of darkness to another, and then back into the main channel door to the dark sea-realm. Every soul journeying to and from time and sea appeared to be frantically seeking for the way out of darkness. However, once they entered the realm of time they all seemed to walk in the opposite direction. Once they enter the time realm they seem bent on entering all the wrong doors that only lead from one darkness realm to another. Although, some have entered the wrong door and are in deep darkness, they believe they are full of light and making freedom progress from the sea-world prison only to find themselves back in their sea-prison- cell once they take their exit from the world. In the time-realm, many are simply walking around in circles of revolving doors of darkness, busy chasing one another in evil heart or passionately pursuing vanity all for nothing.

From witnessing these mysteries unravelling before my very eyes, I became heavily burdened in my realisation of the depth of human ignorance. I felt so much compassion for my vulnerable fellow human beings who although are prisoners of time, consider themselves experts on the things of life. I thought of every human being as a child that thinks they know where they are going even though they have no idea where they are. In open eyes of the spirit, I saw that every human has two aspects; one aspect remains in the dark world of the spiritual sea, whilst the other journeys to the visible surface. The ways of humans in the time-realm is against the true wishes of their other aspect that is in the sea. Once in the realm of time, humans simply become enemies to their sea aspect and everything they do, unless they find the way out of both, the sea and time-realm will only work to keep their total aspect imprisoned still. I also saw in the time-realm, many journeying around, trying to explore the galaxy, but the galaxy is made up of realms and no human can make any spiritual journey progress in their physical journeying round the galaxy with physical equipments. The journey is a soul journey and the soul can only go from one realm to another if the soul has the password for the doors that leads from one realm to the other. Humans with their physical equipment are stationary in one place in their soul, but believe they are making progress in their life-journey.

Although the objectives of the souls journeying to the time-realm is to find the door leading out of darkness, once they enter the realm of time, they end up focusing on entering all the wrong doors which only lead back to the sea-realm. I saw many souls going in and out of the several spiritual doors that are in the realm of time. I noted that even though some of the spiritual doors in the realm of time are wide open, a spirit cannot just simply enter the open door but can only gain access when it is their turn to enter. I saw multitude of spirits waiting outside such doors anxiously struggling to enter. However, no matter what they did they simply could not get in.

The realm of time is a world of spiritual warfare and I saw that every human has many sea opponents whose antics are simply to prevent the human aspect that is in time from finding their way out from both sea and time-realms. I saw that many are unconscious of the attacks and while many are jubilantly rich in the time-realm, they are extremely sad and sorrowful in their sea prison. I saw that in the spirit-realm of time and sea, everything is about POWER. Every spirit is in search of power to dominate, and are looking everywhere for it. I saw desperate faces frantically searching for power and ready to do anything to obtain this power from the sea spirits.

They did not care what they had to do to get it and in their determination, they freely traded with the sea spirits, which are their enemies to the greater disadvantage of their souls. They surrender their entire power of free will to their sea enemies who turn them into robots and control their minds in extreme evil. Under extreme evil control, they sink further into the sea and their sorrow and pain increases. The real picture of sea and time that I was seeing was a very sad one, because although everyone has journeyed to time to find the door that leads away from sea and time, they all seemed to only be in mind of preventing each other from finding the way out.

As all these things continued unfolding before my eyes, the doctor that gave me the pen and paper to write entered to inform me that they would soon let me go, but before they do, they must have a case conference with me. However, I heard her silently say, "We certainly cannot let you go now. You know too much and there is an order from the heads to keep you here". At this stage, my human side just took over and I broke down in tears because I was really feeling too tired and fed up. I'd had enough and all I wanted was to just leave the hospital and go back to my normal life. I did not want to see anything or hear anything anymore. It was just overwhelmingly too much for me to cope with and I sobbed like I had not done before since it all started. As I began to sob uncontrollably, I saw thundering rain begin to fall and the doctor rushed out of the room, saying I should not cry because she will see to it that I am discharged soon. Strangely, I saw many patients also weeping including several members of the hospital staff and silently, I heard many voices say, "Please do not cry for the Lord's wrath is too much in this place".

I saw that hell was in so much heat and deep-heated consuming fire was burning the inhabitants of hell. I saw the principality-heads appear to the surface from the bottomless pits of hell to tell the World Order to let me go. But it now seemed as if the World Order was no longer working for the principality-heads but for their own purpose. They did not seem to hear each other anymore. As all this was going on, I saw patients walking around painfully in circles and I heard the spirits in them saying, "Please let her go, this place is too hot". I saw everyone run up and down and suddenly I saw all the World Order faces, in extreme pain and sorrow and simultaneously they all bowed and said: 'Jesus is Lord'. Immediately afterward, I saw the word 'Victory' written with fire manifested simultaneously in both time and sea across the entire cosmos-order of the dark sea-realms. As soon as the word 'Victory' appeared, both the door to the sea-realm and time-realm disappeared. Now there was only one door, directly in front of me.

I saw that this door was the Lord Jesus Himself and I was right before Him. I saw His face shining all over me. I saw His hands appear, indicating to me that I should enter. As I entered I found myself fully back in His glorious and beautiful presence and He said to me:

Now you are ready to go into the world and preach the Gospel to all creatures and I will be with you even to the end of days. Focus on goodness and be certain that all is well that has already ended well. Your victory is total victory, because those that are victorious in the spirit-realms are victorious in all dominion and dimensional realms. Always be good on deeds and hold on to your everlasting victory. The things that you have seen are not by your might and power but it is so that, you would know that you have a God that is Lord of Victory everlastingly. I have revealed the mysteries of life to you so you would give it as a memorial testimony to the generations of the world.

I am the Alpha and the Omega and as Alpha and Omega the King of revelation. I have revealed all these secrets to you for the benefit of the whole of mankind, so that they would not all perish in their ignorance. No one can see these things unless I open their eyes to see and I opened your eyes to see all that you have seen for the benefit of the human souls. No one can enter unless through I AM, the Door.
No one can shut the door that I have opened and no one can

open the door that I have shut. If you all seek Me, you will find Me. Knock with a repentant heart and the Almighty I AM shall let you enter. If 'I Am' is in you, then no spirit of death can enter into you. Whosoever is in Me is where I Am, and whosoever I Am in is at the heart of My Kingdom, hence darkness can no longer rise against them. My Kingdom is of light and when light comes darkness must disappear. The sea shall pass away and all spirits of the sea in time will pass away forever with it. This is the moment that you must all seek to enter by the straight line, for only through the straight line will you find your way to the gate of eternal life. If you do not follow the straight line, you will perish in the circle of death. Seek in your spirit and not your flesh, and you shall find Me as the Way, the Truth and Life.

You are all blind as flesh and in your blindness you are enemies of your own spirit. I, Jesus came to crucify the flesh in order to make way for you in the spirit. But if you continue to walk in your flesh, you will never find Me as the Way, the Truth and life. O Israel, the door is open and if you seek in repentant heart of the spirit, you will find Me as Your only way of coming out of darkness and entering into light. I am the light of the world and it is time for you to come out of darkness and enter into Me as your Ark of Salvation. For once My ark door of salvation shuts you cannot enter into the Kingdom again. I, Christ, I am the door and no one comes to the Father except through me. Let the buyer beware and let those that have ears hear, for the sea and time shall pass away, but I, Jesus live forever.

This is My message to you all, repent before time runs out.

Cease from your evil and wicked ways. For what no human can see, I see clearly. I shall soon return to give unto every human according to his or her ways. I am the Alpha and Omega, the One Who is, Who was and ever shall be. Blessed are the saints amongst you. Persevere for your reward is everlastingly great. Grace to you, all saints and blessed are your names in Me forever and ever. All the saints say, 'Amen'.

Immediately, after He finished speaking, I saw the entire 'City of light' appear again. The picture was clearer than before and I clearly saw that I was once again, back in the realm of light. I saw a multitude of angels around me. Soon afterwards, the hospital rushed through my discharge process and it was as if they could not wait to get me out! After what seemed like beyond eternity in a hospital mental ward, I finally walked through the doors of the hospital into total and perfect freedom. I had physical bruises and marks all over my body, but it no longer mattered because I knew that the real mark that I carry is the perfect 'life mark' of Jesus. I felt like a victorious soldier on her way to a great homecoming after defeating all her enemies right from within their own territories. My mind was full of peaceful rest. With perfect conviction in my mind that I have everlasting victory by the Name and power of Jesus Christ, I had total confidence that at my mentioning of the Name of Jesus, all knees will surely bow and all tongues in heaven and on earth will always confess that Jesus Christ is Lord of my soul in all dominion and dimensional realms.

The hospital upon my discharge gave me a bag full of medications to take home with me on the basis that I might just need them, but I threw them all away. I had all the medicine I needed the everlasting sweetness love of God. The Lord showed me these things for a memorial testimony from generation to generation till the end of days. He said that the World Order of humans in the end-times would become increasingly and extremely wicked and that they would try to lead the whole world to the bottom of the dark world of the sea. However, our God is Merciful and Faithful and in His faithfulness, He promised He would forgive whosoever repents and give them His Power to resist and overcome the evil poison of the World Order.

My spiritual revelation experience lasted for about three weeks and a bit. But it felt as if it was for a period without end! I was without food for most of the period of my revelations—but God, through His power—kept me strong all through. To Him be all the glory, the honour and the power. Although my spiritual revelation experience only lasted for three weeks or so, my trials in the physical world, in the "natural" continued non-stop, long after I was released from the hospital. Despite my spiritual victory, the spirits of the world carried on testing and trying me on every aspects of my natural life. They tried to make me think that my revelation was nothing but symptoms of madness. They have tried so hard to convince me that my entire revelation is nothing more than manifestations of madness illusions that I am yet to recover from—therefore still in need of ongoing serious psychological help. Many times they used their confusion tactics with the intent of getting me to believe that all that the Lord revealed to me are mere objects of my imagination. They used their weapon of provocation to activate 'flesh' anger in me and tried so hard to frustrate me in my ministerial mission.

Having faced so many continuous trials, I have come to the conclusion in my mind that as long as I exist as a human being on this earth, I will have trials and tribulations. During my relentless trials, I have on several occasions pleaded with the Lord (out of desperation) to allow the death of my natural being, so that I could begin to fully enjoy my spiritual freedom with Him in entirety. The Lord, of course refused to end my journey until my mission is accomplished. And just as He promised, He has always been there to comfort and take me through my daily trials.

I know without a doubt that Jesus is the lover of my soul and as lover of my soul, that He is Lord over my soul everlastingly—regardless of trials. Contrary to the wicked desires of the evil hell spirits of the world in trying me endlessly, I became even more convinced of the Lord's love and in my ever growing conviction, I have continued to see my revelation experience as the highest expression of God's love and grace for my life. The evil spirits of the world know for certain that my soul belongs to Jesus and in Jesus' Mighty Name, I will remain forever victorious—no matter my natural situation or circumstance.

Although Man in his dead state in the time-realm is ignorant of the fact that Christ as RIGHTEOUSNESS is the Way, Truth and Life; the evil spirits of the world know that Jesus as Lord is the only one with the power of resurrection as the 'RESURRECTION'. For the fact that they know Christ is the only Way to eternal Life, the number one objective of the antichrist spirits of the world is to deny Man the opportunity of hearing the Gospel, and so prevent the soul from resurrecting from death. The Gospel is the power of salvation to our souls and it is the only message every spirit in the world came to receive, so as to make the transition from darkness to light. God made way for us to have the Gospel in His continuous demonstration of His faithful love for mankind. No one can stand in the way of the

Gospel, not even the evil spirit of the world. The Gospel of salvation shall spread to the end of the world and once the Gospel is preached in the natural to all unsaved souls, Jesus shall return to judge the world.

The Lord has greatly privileged me by making me a messenger of the Gospel. I thank the Almighty God of the universe for choosing me to witness to the world that Jesus Christ, as Lord is the only door that leads to eternal life. Christ as the only door is Lord over the universal manor. As a witness of life chosen by God the Creator to bear witness of the Truth, speaking in all honesty and truth, I solemnly declare and testify that Jesus Christ is indeed the Way, Truth and Life. I am all that I am because of who He is. He is head above all principalities and powers and when all powers fail and disappear into nothing, His power of love, light and life is the only power that stands everlastingly—now and forevermore. The world is a world of the wicked and evil and unless a spiritual human being submits to Christ's perfect being as the highest power of life in eternal life, the spirit will have no chance against the wicked spirits of the sea that keeps on journeying back and forth from the spiritual sea to the world. Jesus Christ as Lord of the universal manor revealed these things to me to perfect me as a witness of life, to bear accurate testimony of Him as the only One that has the power of salvation, deliverance and redemption. Jesus Christ as Lord is the light of the world and whosoever is not in Him is in the thick darkness of the world.

Christ as the King of kings and 'keeper' of all secrets revealed these things and enabled me to write them down as a testimony of Truth, for the deliverance of souls from lies and for the perfection of the saints throughout the generations of mankind. I am a witness of Jesus Christ, the Resurrection of life.

God took me to His Holy Mountain and gave me the Gospel as a blessing to my soul and also to afford the benefit unto other souls that are willing to receive and repent from their sinful ways. The Gospel is the power of salvation to our souls and the true Gospel is the Gospel of resurrection. God gave us the Gospel of resurrection to preach it to the world, for the resurrection of our souls and also for the perfection of His divine faith in our hearts. Faith comes by hearing, and hearing by the Word of God. Whosoever receives the Word of God with gladness shall find God's grace and shall enjoy God's eternal life's love. Let those who have ears hear.

I pray God will shine His graceful light upon you—the readers of this book and that He enables you to have perfect understanding of what you have read. I also pray He orders your steps and inclines your ears to the true Gospel of Jesus Christ. And that He affords you the power that is in His Word of Truth—the Bible—for the perfection of your souls, for eternal life abiding with His Holy Spirit.

To reaffirm my revelation victory and His purpose for my life, God paved the way for me to have another revelation episode from end of December 2004 through to first week of January 2005. To God be the glory, Freedom House International Ministries was officially born on earth in the year 2005, following that revelation experience. However, since the establishment of Freedom House, the antichrist spirits of the world have consistently tried me and have persistency worked through natural human beings to scatter the ministry. To God be the glory, Freedom House by the special grace of God, continues to remain strong and dedicated to performing the missionary purpose of God in accordance with the predestined will of God for it as a ministry.

Having experienced all that I have experienced and having seen all that I have seen, I have come to realise that every flesh is my enemy, including my own flesh. From witnessing all that I have witnessed, I know for certain that if it were not for God's grace, I would be unable to exist as a 'normal' human being for the rest of my days in time. I am forever thankful to God for settling me back in the 'natural' world, to have a relatively normal human life. I thank God everyday for enabling me to still relate to my fellow human beings, bearing in mind that He lifted their veil cover for me to see that the flesh being behind every facemask is my spiritual enemy.

Following my revelation experience—in order to settle me down into human society for the essence of fulfilling my purpose—God highlighted to me that He had not revealed the secrets of life to me so that I would live my natural existence in complete isolation from all human beings. Rather, He revealed life secrets to me to afford me perfect understanding, to make me His all round perfect witness.

I thank the Lord each day for enabling me to walk in proper spiritual discernment of the things I have seen and continue to see with my spiritual eyes. I exalt His Holy Name forever, for shielding me with His protective wall of 'fire' from the constant wicked darts and arrows of the wicked invisible spirits that are hibernating in the sinful body of Man in the darkness-world of sin. I thank Him for giving my soul power to daily resist the wiles of the devil and glorify His Name for His daily spiritual loving affections towards me. I reverence His Holy Name for striping the devil naked before my very eyes and I thank Him for affording me knowledge of life through His revelations to me.

I worship my Father in heaven for giving me His overcoming

authority and power and I bless His Holy Name for enabling my mind to daily reject the wrong signals of the wicked. I thank the King of glory for leading and directing my mind daily to continue walking in faith with His Holy Spirit. I thank You Christ, my everlasting Redeemer for justifying me fully on the account of Your own RIGHTEOUSNESS. I thank You my God for Your grace and faithfulness. I am saved not by my will or power, but by Your grace, O faithful God. I owe You my all and from now on to eternity, my soul will always remain in total submission and surrender unto He that is my Lord of victory everlastingly. To the Trinity God the Father, God the Son and God the Holy Ghost be all honour, all glory and all power, always now and forevermore. Amen.

CHAPTER NINE
THE DEVIL IS A LIAR

"Who is a liar but he that denieth that Jesus is the Christ? He is antichrist, that denieth the Father and the Son. Whosoever denieth the Son, the same hath not the Father: but he that acknowledgeth the Son hath the Father also".

—1 John 2:22-23

The world is full of mysteries and it is only by grace of revelation that we can find the answers to all our questions. Through His revelations to me, God opened my eyes to see the world for what it is. In open eyes of the spirit, I saw that the world is an adversarial spiritual courtyard and every man on earth is a witness of the spirit that is on their inside. The adversarial world of Man is a world of two main conviction barriers that are there to prevent us all from finding the truth about God. The first main barrier is that God does not exist and if you manage to cross this first barrier, the second is that even though He exists, He hates you. The first mission of the devil's advocates on earth is to convict the spirit in the former, so that the spirit remains in total darkness and ignorance of God's existence. If a spirit makes it through the first barrier, the second mission is to convict a believer that God hates him or her, through bombarding the believer with world trials and tribulations. The only One that can bring down both barriers and convince us of His perfect Truth is Christ Jesus; God in Person revealed.

No one can bear witness to God's existence and of His divine love outside of God. God is the Truth and no one can have conviction of the truthfulness of God in darkness mind of death. In the fall of man, death convicted the spirit of Man in lies and as a result, Man hates the truthfulness of God with deep passion. We know God as the Truth and believe in His Word of Truth not because we have physically heard or seen God outside of ourselves, but because we feel His presence within us. We can never find the true God if we concentrate our minds on finding evidence of God's existence outside of us. God is Spirit and as such, invisible to the ordinary eyes. It is only through revelation of Himself to our spirit being, that we will be able to know who He is, was and ever shall be. God reveals Himself by enabling us to have a one on one relationship with Him. Through our personal relationship with God, we experience God's true love for us. In experiencing His true love, we are able to overcome entire barriers of the darkness-world, which is that God does not exist or even if He does exist, He hates us.

A person that has no personal relationship experience with God cannot comprehend in their mind how it would be possible to have such relationship. Most people will not only find it difficult to understand that one can have a personal relationship with God, but will consider it madness when we say God 'speaks' to us and we can 'hear' Him speak. Communication is a central aspect of a relationship so if God does not speak to us, making it possible for us to hear Him, we cannot consciously say we have a personal 'relationship' with Him. Due to the fact that our relationship with God takes place within us, no one but us has concrete proof of the true nature and extent of our personal relationship with Him. Except God manifests His Holy nature and character as evidence of His presence in us, no other can see that we have a one on one relationship with the Holy God, no matter how hard we try to convince them.

God as a Spirit is Holy Spirit and we bear record and witness of God's love and of His Holy eternal existence as living souls and spirits in Him. The carnally minded in the world will always try to confuse the mind not to believe in the truthfulness of God's existence and of His love for us. To be carnal minded is to carry a burden of confusion. Those who carry a confusion 'burden' will always have an everyday, irresistible yearn and desire to make false submissions to the world-courtyard that there is no evidence that God exists or that He loves us.

The carnally minded can only succeed in deceiving their unsaved counterparts. This is because the living requires no further evidence of God's existence or of His love because all the evidence that we need is already on the inside of us once we are saved—which is the Holy Spirit of God. Once we have evidence of God's existence and love inside us, the devilish spirits will heavily try our flesh to make us believe that God hates us based upon what He is allowing us to go through. The advocates of the devil are advocates of lies. Although they will go to any length to try to convince the mind that there is no God, they are unable to provide any convincing evidence to back their false claims because such evidence does not exist. It is therefore impossible to provide evidence that is nonexistent to disproof the existence of the self-existing God. The evidence of God's existence is God Himself. God existed before anyone came into being and we all came into existence through Him. As such, unless He gives Himself to us as evidence of His existence and of

His love for us, the soul will remain in darkness of God's true existence and of His divine loving nature.

The evidence that a devil's advocate will attempt to give of God not being in existence is in his actual words of false submissions such as, "There is no evidence that God exists". This of course is just a blank statement to distract many from believing in the true testimony of God's own witnesses. A real life advocate knows that understanding the evidence is what leads to proper submissions and the result of proper submissions are real life soul convictions. The game of the devil's advocate is to make his false submission his evidence so that the mind remains convicted in the wrong submission that has no evidence to support it. As such, it will not make any difference that there is lack of evidence to support the false claims since the mind is already convinced in the false submission, even though there is no evidence to support it. The entire game of the devil's advocate is to convince the mind with his carnal submission, which is in itself, the complete lie to prevent people from accepting the true evidence which is; that God was, is and ever shall be the eternal self-existing God.

A person in wrong conviction is a puppet and agent of the devil and as agents of the devil laden with a heavy burden to convince others that his wrong convictions are true facts of life. Such persons will attempt to discharge their heavy 'confusion' burden unto others by just affirming the 'no evidence' submission, which is the lie in itself. When challenged by others to defend his or her false submission (opinion) with some realistic evidence, he or she will maliciously shift the burden of defence unto the side of the true witness to make him/her appear as the liar. Irrespective of the amount of clear evidence from the true witness, the devil's agent will show his or her final contempt for the truth by simply affirming his submission that there is 'no evidence' that there is God.

The devil's advocates know for sure that to be convinced in a submission that is total lie, is to reject any truthful evidence on the basis that it is all a lie. The ultimate aim of the devil's advocate is to convince the mind in false submission to deny the soul the truth. If evidence leads to submission and submission to conviction, then to believe in a submission that is without spiritual evidence to support it, is to always be in mind to disapprove of true spiritual evidence. Except by the grace of God, it is ordinarily impossible to free a person from their wrongful soul conviction, no matter how hard we try to make them see the true evidence. To believe in lies is to be in bondage of death and to be in bondage of death is to be a puppet of the evil forces. Except God by His graceful mercies convicts the soul with true evidence of His love for us, the soul will remain in bondage to the lies. The Gospel is the Truth and it is for this reason that the evil spirits of the world do not wish for any human being to hear it, let alone embrace it. God made way in His infinite mercies for us to hear the Gospel of salvation and that whosoever hears and willingly receives it would no longer be subject to the evil and wicked oppressions of the darkness spirits of the world.

The carnally minded is the devil's vessel and as such evilly persistent in their world-courtyard mission to convince the mind into wrongful submission. To have wrong conviction is to be openly subject to abusive relationships with the spirits of death and the entire aim of the devil is to abuse the vulnerable human being. The devil's advocates are persistent in their evil mission because they carry a burden of confusion to confuse the world. They have a daily irresistible urge to discharge their burden of confusion onto the world and they will stop at nothing, in trying to convince the world that there is no God or that even if we find that He does exist, that He hates us. The more God reveals Himself to us, the louder the devil's advocates will sound the hell bell of lies in the deaf ears of the blind humans to try and harden their hearts further in lies.

Therefore my godly word of wisdom to all is, 'Let buyer beware'. Because whosoever follows the devil's advocates will lose their case before God on the day of final judgement. The devil is a liar and because he is a liar, he has lost his entire case before God and whosoever advocates for the devil is automatically a loser before God. To fall for the lies of the devil's advocates is to remain guilty of sin and those that are guilty of sin will end up losers just like Satan, from the beginning to the end.

"But the natural man receiveth not the things of the Spirit of God: for they are foolishness unto him: neither can he know them, because they are spiritually discerned".
—1 Corinthians 2:14

God is life and to say God does not exist is a direct admittance by a person that they are spiritually dead. The spiritually dead—that unsaved cannot be true witnesses of God because to be dead is to lack knowledge of who God is, was and ever will be. Only the saved—the living can bear the same record and witness that God bore of Himself. Only God can raise us from spiritual death back to life and place us in His presence to bear the same record and testimony that He bore of Himself. We can only know the true nature of God when we are in a conscious, spiritual relationship with Him. No one can enter into relationship with God except God Himself makes it possible for it to happen. Those that God has separated from Himself can have no knowledge of life and as such can only bear record and testimony of the spirits of death that resides in them.

The carnally minded is a devil's advocate that is in the world-courtyard to testify and witness against God to bury the minds of people in deeper darkness and ignorance of godly truth. If anyone seeks evidence of God in a carnal mindset, he or she will never have evidence of God's eternal love and perfect life existence. To be carnally minded is to be dead and the dead cannot testify to God's existence because God is a God of the living and not the dead. God is love and God as love is a God of spiritual eternal life relationships. My evidence of God's existence is based on the fact that His Holy Spirit dwells in me and I am in a conscious relationship with Him every day through His Holy Spirit of life. As such, I need not look for further evidence of God's existence outside of myself because all the evidence that I need of His existence and love for me is actually inside me. Inside His Holy Spirit, I experience His love every day and I am convinced in my soul of His undying love for me. God as love is my Redeemer and as my Redeemer, Comforter of my soul. God is WORD and His oracle Word of life is deep in my soul to comfort and empower me daily to overcome my trials and in overcoming them, remain in soul conviction of His love for me no matter what I go through.

No deceitful, carnal words can change my God given spiritual conviction because the true Word of God lives within my spirit and as such—carnal lies cannot dominate or confuse my spiritual mind. The testimony I bear of God is of His Holy Spirit as Love and this is the same testimony that God bore of Himself that He is Love. My testimony of God's existence and of

His love for me is something that I am only able to bear in my personal relationship with Him. No one can bear record of God's love except through a personal relationship with His Holy Spirit of love. A testimony, which is of the Holy Spirit, is reality. But that which is of the flesh is nothing but carnal illusions. From revealing Himself to me, I have found that God is wonderfully Merciful and I consider it necessary to daily humble myself before Him.

Through God's Holy spiritual knowledge and perfect life revelations, I am now aware that in the body of sin I walked in convictions of lies. But by grace, God justified me through the atonement blood of Christ and totally freed me from the entire bondage of lies. The knowledge of God's graceful justification is not knowledge of the flesh, but of heaven. And no one that is of the flesh can have the understanding of this heavenly knowledge. Except God by His grace convicts our souls with His real life knowledge, His divine knowledge of life will seem as foolishness or some crazy idea. Knowledge of God is knowledge of life-secrets.

The entire realm of life is full of secret knowledge and information that no one can just 'stumble' into, by any means. This is because God is life and the entire secrets of life are on the inside of Him. Unless God reveals what is on His inside for us to see, no one can force their way into the inside of God to see the secrets. God only lets us in on His eternal life secrets for witnessing and testimonial purposes. No man in sinful darkness can recognise God for who He is and unless God reveals Himself, no one can know Him, even if He were to be standing right before our very eyes. God only reveals Himself to us to account the record of His spiritual goodness and love to us, so that we are able to testify of His goodness and love unto others that are yet to have that knowledge.

The testimony of God's love for us is the message of eternal life, hope and salvation and as such: Good News. God's Word, which is the Good News of the Bible, is our key to finding the truthfulness of God. The Gospel is the Good News because it is the news of resurrection from death, and to resurrect our souls from death is the whole essence of Christ coming to the world as the Resurrection Himself. God by His special grace elected me, convicted my soul with His knowledge of life, and opened my eyes to see the secrets of life; to bear record and testimony of it all as the whole truth unto all nations in this crucial end-time.

God opened the door of life's secrets to me out of His grace for the benefit of the salvation of the souls of mankind. In opening the door of life's secret, God opened my spiritual eyes to see that the universe is a realm of light and darkness and only one secret door leads from darkness to light and this secret door, which is really not a secret is Christ. The eternal abode of God is His Kingdom of light and the door that leads to His everlasting Kingdom is Christ. We cannot find the secret door that leads to God's eternal Kingdom of life, let alone enter through our ordinary search, unless God opens our spiritual eyes to see the door and guides us to enter. No one can see the door or force their way into God's Kingdom of light without revelation by His grace.

God will only give us access to eternal life secrets by His Grace for the sake of His Glory. By His grace, God opened my spiritual eyes to see that the real journey that Man is involved in, is a soul journey. Soul travelling is like travelling through many radio frequencies and several television channels from the same spot. Just like television and radio, you cannot see what is on other channels or hear what is on another radio frequency unless you change the channel to another channel or the radio frequency to another. The spiritual picture and sound signal that a person gets in the world depends on which spiritual channel or frequency they are tuned into. If it is the channel of death, they will only get wrong signals and if it is life, they will get all the right signals. Once a person locks his or her mind in the right channel and is constantly receiving the right picture and sound signals, they will have power to resist any interruption attempt from the channels of death to replace their right signals with wrong signals.

A person can only change their spiritual channel frequency from death to life through entering the only door that leads from darkness to light. Finding and entering the door of life is the entire mission and purpose of every man's journey to earth. Whosoever finds the door of life (Christ) shall enter the realm of light through the door, for He is also light. A soul would only have successfully completed their entire life's mission when they enter the right door and through that door, enter into the glorious light presence of God. Only if a person understands the deep secret within this revelation will his or her soul realistically begin the real life-journey of finding freedom from the realm of darkness to the realm of light.

Life is full of secrets. The foundation and height of all secrets is in the heavenly light-realm of God. To afford me perfect understanding of the door to heaven, God took me on my universal, spiritual soul journey and opened my spiritual eyes to see beyond my human comprehension. In my unforgettable journey, God opened my eyes to see that the universe is a realm of gateways and no one can go in and out of a realm except through the gateway that leads in and out of the realms. God opened my eyes to see that the world-realm is a realm of endless darkness corridors, with many side doors that only lead the soul back to the darkness dungeon. The original realm of Man was the realm of light but sin automatically shut the door of light on the face of Man and placed Man inside the realm of darkness to become prisoners of evil principality-angels. The world is a realm of time and it is full of several deadly revolving doors of darkness. Unless a spirit finds and enters the door to the realm of light, the soul will only journey round and round in circles of death in the darkness dungeon realms.

Although the hands of time seem like they are moving and as such seems as if time is constantly changing, the spiritual truth is that time itself does not move forward but only goes round and round in circles. The time-realm is a spiritual darkness prison and no one can escape or free him/herself from the realm of time no matter how hard they try. Every spiritually dead soul that is in the prison of time is not making any spiritual, soul progress; instead they are only going round and round in the circles of time—in and out of the dungeon of death. Only if a person finds and enters the right door, will they become free from a back and forth journey in the circles of time and death.

The mission of every man to Earth is to find the One and only door that leads from darkness to light because without finding and entering the door the soul will remain a prisoner in death. Only through God's grace do we have access to the one door that leads from the realm of darkness back to the realm of light. Unless God opens our eyes to see this door and enables us to enter, no man can see or enter, to be able to find their way from the realm of darkness back to the realm of light. Since time is a realm of darkness, the journey of Man in time is all in thick darkness. Unless we submit our souls unto God to lead us in our journey, no man can journey out of darkness back to the kingdom light of God.

Everyone is on a soul journey to find the way back to the homeland of God. Without the help of God, no soul can find their way from darkness back to the kingdom light of God. Since the beginning of time, the devil and his angels have been busy erecting their barriers of lies in the path of man's journey. They have continued to do so from generation to generation to prevent Man from finding the only door that will lead their soul from darkness to light. God as the Creator of all, is life and as life, the Word of entire truth. God brought the door of life from the invisible to the visible and by so doing demolished every barrier of lies, which is that, "God does not exist or that if He exists He hates us". Whosoever enters the right door will find the undisputable evidence of God's existence—which is the Holy Spirit of God. When we enter that door and through the Holy Spirit of God, the devil can no longer deceive us by propagating that God does not exist or that He hates us. This is because the evidence of God's existence and love for us is already in our soul which is God Himself.

The devil is a liar and no matter how long a lie goes on, it will never be the truth. God reveals Himself as the whole truth through making His door visible to us. Unless you enter that door, you will continue to fall victim to the wicked lies of the devil. God as the Truth convicts our souls with the true evidence of Himself by giving us His Holy Spirit to enable our souls make the rightful submission to His Spirit of life. We are only conscious of God's existence and of His divine love when we are inside His Holy Spirit. That is why the entire game of the devil is to deny Man reconciliation with the Holy Spirit of God. To be without God's Holy Spirit is to be dead and a dead spirit cannot bear testimony of God's love. The revelation account you have read in this book is hard evidence that no devil can dispute no matter how hard they try.

The revelations in this book are spiritual evidence and not carnal, so if you consider it from a carnal perspective you will remain blindfolded by the illusionist devil. However, if you have read the entire revelations in this book with open mind of the spirit you will be convinced by the true evidence therein. The evidence of truth in this book is corroborated by the evidence of truth in the Holy Bible; the only book that contains the whole truth. The devil's number one aim as an enormous liar is to discredit the witness through acts of provocation, accusations and also scare people with threats of death or incarceration to prevent them from openly witnessing of Christ as the truth and RESURRECTION. The devil knows that if a spirit that is dead is afraid of death or incarceration, then that spirit has no chance of resurrecting from its spiritual death or becoming free from eternal death imprisonment.

'The wages of sin is death' (Romans 6:23) and to remain dead on Judgement Day is to automatically be guilty of sin. The only way to resurrect from spiritual death is to fear God because the fear of God is the beginning of wisdom. To fear God Himself is the only means of defeating the evil dead because God is the only One that has power to condemn a soul permanently to death and also resurrect a soul from death. The devil, as the first and last to sin against God is forever condemned by God to be evil on deeds and as evil on deeds, sentenced by God to remain eternally dead without parole. The devil as a condemned evildoer is an eternal loser and those who follow the devil will never resurrect from death, but die as doers of evil to perish with the devil in his graveyard of wickedness forever and ever. This is a revelation like never before in our time, all for the glory of the God who the devils says is not, but, who really is, was and ever shall be the self-existing, Creator Uncreated Supreme Head of the universe. Those who say He is not are the ones that are not and they say He is not, because they are spiritually dead and as the dead, they are NOTHING but dead liars.

CHAPTER TEN

TO GOD BE THE GLORY

"And the Word was made flesh, and dwelt among us, (and we beheld his glory, the glory as of the only begotten of the Father,) full of grace and truth. John bare witness of him, and cried, saying, This was he of whom I spake, He that cometh after me is preferred before me; for he was before me. And of his fulness have all we received, and grace for grace. For the law was given by Moses, but grace and truth came by Jesus Christ".

—John 1: 14-17

The world is like a motion picture divinely created and orchestrated by God. He is the director of life. Unless we seek Him in mind of relationship it will be impossible for us to identify our roles, let alone play them. God, as the director of life is the Creator of all and if in our human world we have rulers and leaders, it is total foolishness to think that our universe that is so huge and complex in its functionality is without a ruling head. A person that says God does not exist is actually saying, that he or she is a 'god' in his own right therefore only subject to his own self-governing rules. To say that you are only subject to your own self-governing rules is to consider yourself as one with absolute power and authority, to dictate and define everything according to your own personal will and desires.

If the universe predates human beings, then it cannot be right to say or think that humans have absolute power and authority over every universal matter and affair. If humans exist in a planet where they have no control over events of the next second, how then can it be possible for humans to have supremacy over a universe that they have no control over its functions and operations? Life is only worth living in the presence of the goodness of God, and judging from human history of unending violence, war and unrest in the world—the result of human self-governing has been mainly generational evil and widespread injustice.

The supreme order of life is goodness, not evil. Goodness is light and evil is darkness. If Man, through self-governance is not capable of achieving overall goodness on earth, then human order which is entire darkness cannot be the final universal order. The universe is powered by light and as such subject to the ruling power of light. To be the supreme head and ruler of the universe is to have power and control over all elements of the universe and also the absolute capability of making all things work together for the sake of goodness. God is love and as love—light. As light He is always good on deeds. As good on deeds, God is love and as love the self-existing Creator Uncreated, Most High Ruler of the universe and the all in all Head. God is always more than able to make all things work together as light for the goodness sake of life. God as Creator of all is unaccountable to no other but Himself. However, as the Divine and universal ruler, God always holds Himself accountable to His own Word. God as the Supreme King and Ruler of the universe, is, was and ever shall be. No one is a living soul outside of God because He is Life and as Life the only source of true life.

From finding and having a close and personal relationship with God, my soul is at peace because to find the one true God is to find the answers to life's entire questions. To be without God is to have no knowledge of who we are, where we are or where we are headed. I was a lost sheep that needed to be with my Shepherd, because on my own I had no way of finding my way through the thick darkness of the world. To God be the glory as my Shepherd, by His special grace He found and saved me from eternal hell damnation. God, by His special grace revealed heaven and hell to me not just for the sake of revelation, but also for the purpose of giving me a perfect testimony of the Truth to give to the world in this crucial end-time.

Heaven and hell are real and having experienced both in the manner that I did, I do not think anyone in their right mind would truly want to miss heaven and end up in hell. Most people including unbelievers, upon the death of their loved ones always seem to find consolation in the notion that their loved ones have gone to heaven or a better place of permanent rest. The fact that people are in this mind of thinking, is evidence that they believe heaven is a place of rest and hell is a place of pain and sorrow that they must avoid ending up in. People not only believe heaven is a good place to end up in, they also take solace in the idea that they will join their loved ones there one day when they too take their leave from this world. The question is: How can anyone be sure that their loved ones have made it to heaven or that they will join them there one day? The answer is: No one is sure of ending up in heaven except they are born again, John 3:3-7:

"Jesus answered and said unto him [Nicodemus], 'Verily, verily I say unto thee, except a man be born again, he cannot see the kingdom of God'. Nicodemus saith unto him, 'How can a man be born when he is old? Can he enter the second time into the mother's womb, and be born'? Jesus answered, 'Verily, verily, I say unto thee, except a man be born of water and of the spirit, he cannot enter into the kingdom of God. That which is born of the flesh is flesh; and that which is born of the Spirit is spirit. Marvel not that I said unto thee, Ye must be born again'".

If we want to end up in heaven and avoid hell, we must start by asking ourselves: How do we find our way to heaven in order to avoid hell? Unless we find the pathway to heaven and avoid the road to hell, the chances of anyone realising their wishes of ending up in heaven are zero. Heaven and hell are life mysteries which only God the Creator can reveal to us. No one can be sure of anything except by soul convincing revelation from God. God is a God of revelation and He reveals life's secrets to us in order to impart His knowledge and wisdom of life unto us. God has so far revealed Himself to me in manners and ways that I never could have thought possible. His revelations to us are not by our works but by His special grace. No one can do anything to earn God's grace because His grace is unmerited favour. I am deeply thankful to Him every day because my soul is convinced that it is by His grace that He opened His door of light to me in order to place me in His revelation of life's secrets, for the sake of His glory.

God is a God of purpose and He reveals His mysteries to us for His Kingdom purpose. God selected me by grace and by grace took me to His Mountain of life to reveal the secrets of life to me. Following these revelations, God sent me back to the world from His Holy Mountain to preach the Gospel of RESURRECTION to the world. Although I am in the world, I am no longer of the world. Whoever is in Christ is no longer of the world, but of the Holy Mountain of God. The Gospel is the power of salvation unto all souls and to receive the Gospel with gladness is to find soul redemption of the spirit. My Gospel message to you O souls of earth from the Holy Mountain is — "Repent! For the Kingdom of God has come and His Will be done forever".

Today my soul rejoices for I am no longer walking in destiny of death but serving my godly predestined purpose for my life, which is to preach the Gospel of salvation unto all nations. If am predestined, then it is all by the grace of Our Lord Jesus Christ. For He, as my Lord and Saviour is the Alpha and Omega, the eternal WORD of life. As WORD, of beginning and the end, He is the light. As light, the Word of resurrection, redemption and the justification that is in the Gospel message that I preach. Whoever receives Christ's Word of light with gladness, Christ Himself, as the living WORD will enter their hearts to become power of salvation in their souls. As for me I have entire evidence of Christ's deliverance POWER and through my revelation experiences, I remain convinced always that greater always is the God in me, than any spirit that is in the world. I am fully convinced through His graceful redemption of my soul that my God is Good and Merciful and that His Goodness and Mercies endures forever. This I know and for I know He is Good, I know for a fact that He will make every good and evil to work together for my predestined purpose in this life and in eternal life forever.

By His special grace, God predestined me before the foundation of the world to be an advocate in Christ. To serve my predestined purpose, He did not allow me to practice Law, which I had studied in carnal mind. For the sake of His glory, He gave me understanding of His divine law of love to preach as the Good News unto all nations. By His special grace, God robed me with His advocacy light-garment and enabled me with His powerful Word of divine salvation to preach it as the Gospel of life unto all creatures across the world. The Christ that I preach is the light of the universe.

As light, He is the resurrection of life and Christ as the resurrection of life—lives forever. I know He lives forever because the same Christ, who came and died for our sins—is alive in me today, now and forever. I preach and confess Him as my personal everlasting Saviour, Holy Redeemer, the Alpha and the Omega God. If Christ is dead, then He cannot be my Redeemer or Saviour. It is for the fact that He lives, that He is my Saviour. As my Saviour, He came and died for my sins, resurrected as life and lives now and forevermore in the glory of His eternal kingdom. At the end of my life's service here on earth, ashes shall go to ashes and dust shall return to dust. However, because I am in Christ and He is in me, my soul is in RESURRECTION. Therefore, the ground shall not keep me down. To be in Christ is to be in God's heart and in God's heart, in God's kingdom. If we are in God's kingdom, then our soul shall never again taste the sting of death, for in Christ Jesus our soul is already in resurrection of life.

Christ as the Alpha and Omega is the only door to heaven and no one can enter the kingdom of God except through Christ as the Lord and Saviour. The whole essence of Christ's remission work and of His electing the saints to preach the Gospel unto all creatures is to make us see that the Christ crucified, is the door to heaven. Christ as the door is the whole essence of the entire revelations by the Father, the Son and the Holy Ghost. God gave us Christ as the key and the door to His heart to enable us make our way to heaven. The entire game of the enemy is to deceive humans with promises of fake wealth. This is so that humans would continue to walk hand in hand with evil and in so doing, lose the focus of their journey purpose to earth, which is to find and enter Christ the door, our Ark of Salvation. Whoever joins hands with evil is in covenant with death and whoever is in covenant with death is a fool. Wisdom is to join hands with Christ because only those that are in Christ are in covenant relationship with God.

God has all wisdom and the evidence of God's wisdom in us is our ability to choose Him as goodness even though we have entire capacity of evil. It is divine wisdom to choose good, out of good and evil because profit in life is only in God as entire Goodness. Those that trade in the mind of evil, trade to have total loss forever. God in His everlasting glory is forever good on deeds and it is only when we choose in the goodness mind of God that He will certify us as His good on deeds wise sons.

God's goodness revealed is Christ and it is only in Christ that we are able to choose goodness and resist evil temptations. Christ as the King of kings and Lord of lords has overcome all evil temptations for us and if we are in Christ, we have overcome, just as He has. Christ as the All in all is the Way, the Truth and the Life and whoever finds Christ has found God. Christ is God's entire Word revealed and the Word of God is the same as God. Whosoever is without Christ is in bondage of lies and only Christ as the Truth can set humans free from the bondage and captivity of devilish lies.

When we preach the Gospel of Christ, it is to release the power of God's Truth to the soul because the Gospel is the power of salvation. As the saints continue to preach the Word of Truth, that Christ is the only door to heaven from now to the end of days, let those that have ears, hear and let those that have eyes, see. This is revelation revealed and as revelation revealed, it is Christ's testimony of life in the end-times to the end of days. All of God's revelation is now opened to our eyes of understanding, to see that Christ in all realms and dominion is the all-powerful and Almighty. Christ as the Almighty is life and if we are in Christ, we have eternal life victory over death. My record and witness of Christ is that He is the only Truth and as the Truth, the Lord of victory everlastingly. Christ is the lover of my soul and my soul in Him is in everlasting victory over death. The crucified Christ is alive in me and as a result, I have all of His eternal life's victory.

The testimony of Christ's love is divine testimony and revelation knowledge of life. If you are in doubt of the TRUE evidence that is in the Holy Bible and this book, it is because you are thinking carnally and the carnal minded can never, have knowledge of God's love as Christ. This is because the knowledge of God's love is divinely spiritual and He will only open the eyes to see Christ as the Truth when the soul is humbly submissive unto Him as the Supreme God and overall Ruling Head of the universe. To be carnal, is to be spiritually dead and those that are dead are without any knowledge of God. The power of life and death belongs to God and God as the ultimate power and Ruler of the universe, is the only One that can resurrect the dead back to life. God gave us Christ as His only begotten Son to resurrect and redeem our souls from death unto His eternal life of peace, rest and everlasting joy. The prophets and all the saints bore witness that Christ is not just a Son of God but God in Person (Isaiah 9:6-7). John the Baptist testified of Christ, as the Lamb of God who came to earth to take our sins away and baptise us with 'fire' and this fire is the Holy Ghost fire of God (John 1:36). The Bible revealed that Christ is the only begotten Son of God and that it is only through Him we can avoid eternal damnation of hell (St. John 3:16). The testimony of Christ is the Spirit of true prophecy (Revelations 19:10). A true prophet operating under the prophetic Spirit of God must bear testimony of Christ as Son of God and as the Son—God in Person. Therefore, whosoever says Christ is not the Son of God and as Son of God—God in person is not a true prophet of God but antichrist spirit (1 John 2:22-29).

Christ as the Son of God knew who He was, is and ever shall be. The entire Scriptures of God, which is the Holy Bible, revealed and confirmed Christ as the only begotten Son of God and as such the Messiah that came from heaven to earth to RESURRECT us from death. In the Gospel account of the Bible, Christ bore testimony of who He is and ever shall be and only those that see Christ for who He says He is and the Father says He is shall be saved. In the Gospel of John for instance, starting from Chapter Six, verse 51 Christ said:

"I am the living bread which came down from heaven: if any man eats of this bread, he shall live forever: and the bread that I will give is my flesh, which I will give for the life of the world".

In John 8:12 Christ said:

"I am the light of the world: he that followeth me shall not walk in darkness, but shall have the light of life".

In John 10:7-9 Christ said:

> "Verily, verily, I say unto you, I am the door of the sheep.
> All that ever came before me are thieves and robbers: but
> the sheep did not hear them. I am the door: by me if any
> man enters in, he shall be saved, and shall go in and out,
> and find pasture".

In John.11: 25, Jesus said:

> "I am the resurrection, and the life: he that believeth in me,
> though he was dead, yet shall he live".

In John.14: 6, Jesus said:

> "I am the way, the truth, and the life; no man cometh unto
> the Father, but by me".

In John 15:1, Jesus said:

> "I am the true vine, and my Father is the husbandman".

My question to you today is: Who do you think Christ is? In
Revelation, Chapter One, verse 18, Christ said:

> " I am he that liveth, and was dead; and, behold, I am alive
> for evermore, Amen; and have the keys of hell and of death".

Hell is at the centre of the earth and the only one that can release a soul from the prison of hell is CHRIST JESUS, being the Only One that has the keys to open and shut the gate of hell. If you are yet to give your life to Christ, then you are without a doubt in Hell on Earth. To avoid ending up locked up in hell permanently, it is important you seek Christ today humbly in your soul and enter into a personal spiritual relationship with Him. Contrary to what the devil will have you believe that there is no God, no Jesus, no hell, no heaven and that there is no such thing as eternal life through Christ, I can honestly confirm from my own firsthand experience that there is God and God in Person is Christ. As God in Person, He is the only one that can redeem a soul from hell and guarantee entrance into heaven.

Christ is alive forever and He is speaking today just as He spoke back then. His Word to you today is that you should search for answers, not in the mind of flesh but in a submissive heart of repentance unto Him and you will find that He is the Truth and the Way to eternal life of peace, rest and joy. Christ as the only door to heaven is today calling you to enter Him and become free from eternal hell damnation and He in essence, says:

> I stand at the door as the only door. If you knock today with a true heart of repentance, I will open the door of my heart for you to enter and receive power to dwell in My eternal life's presence of peace, rest and everlasting joy.

I pray that God by His grace will give your soul perfect understanding of Christ's evidence from His record of revelations, as it is in the Holy Bible and in this book. Christ is forever faithful and today as He is calling you to enter Him as the door, do not turn deaf ears to His call—for tomorrow might be too late. All other doors only lead to eternal hell damnation and from what I have seen hell to be, it is without a doubt, a place to be avoided at all cost.

 Seek answers in heart and mind of the spirit and as you seek, you will certainly find that Jesus Christ is the only door to heaven as the truth and life in eternal life forever. If you are in mind of freedom from HELL ON EARTH, you can signal to Christ from your spiritual prison-cell that you wish to follow Him, to get saved from today onward and be with Him for eternal life in heaven by saying this simple prayer:

> Lord Jesus, I confess with my mouth that I am a sinner and I believe in my heart having heard the evidence from this testimony that You are the Only begotten Son of God that came from heaven to earth to redeem my soul from hell with Your blood of remissions. I ask for Your forgiveness and invite You today to enter my soul, mind, body, heart and spirit and become my personal Lord and Saviour. Count me amongst Your sheep forever and do not allow my soul to perish in hell. Wash me clean with Your atonement blood, release me permanently from hell and align my will with Your Will for goodness sakes of my soul. Order my footsteps in line of Your glorious path and enable me to dwell in Your presence and be counted amongst Your saints at Your Second Coming.

If you have said this prayer in total mind of humility, get ready to be truly tried and tested. Your trial and temptation is necessary for your perfect regeneration and with Christ on your side you shall overcome in all aspects (John 16:33). Christ in His ultimate authority has already overcome the world, and all the darkness realms of hell for all those who are in Him. Upon salvation when we are filled with the Holy Spirit, the Bible teaches that greater is the Christ in you than the antichrist spirits that are in the world (1 John 4:4). Therefore, in all your trials be of a good cheer and remain confident that with Christ on your side, no principalities, powers, rulers of darkness or wickedness in high places can overcome your soul. Unto our God the Father, Son and Holy Ghost I give all the glory, honour and power everlastingly for my soul and your soul. The saints say, "The grace of our Lord Jesus Christ, the love of God and sweet fellowship of the Holy Spirit rest and abide with us now and forevermore. Amen".

Author's Contact

If you have questions or comments about this book, you may contact the author at the email address below.

Pastor Olabisi Obideyi

Email:
freedomhouse7@aol.com
divinegraceent777@gmail.com

Please also check out my ministry websites:
http://www.freedom-house.org.uk
http://www.freedomhouseintministries.com
http://www.freedomhousemedia.com
http://www.encouragedbygod.com
http://www.hopealliance.org.uk
http://www.divinegraceenterprise.com

CPSIA information can be obtained at www.ICGtesting.com
Printed in the USA
BVOW08s0117100315

390991BV00021B/149/P